D0952715

Also by Martha Brockenbrough

It Could Happen to You

Things That Make Us [Sic]

The Society for the Promotion

of Good Grammar

Takes on Madison Avenue,

Hollywood, the White House,

and the World

*

Martha Brockenbrough

ST. MARTIN'S PRESS New York

www.stmartins.com

Text illustrations by Jaime Temairik

BOOK DESIGN BY AMANDA DEWEY

Library of Congress Cataloging-in-Publication Data

Brokenbrough, Martha.
    Things that make us [sic] : the Society for the Promotion of Good
Grammar takes on Madison Avenue, Hollywood, the White House, and the
world / Martha Brokenbrough.—1st ed.
             p. cm.
   ISBN-13: 978-0-312-37808-0
   ISBN-10: 0-312-37808-4
  1. English language—Usage.   2. English language—Errors of usage.
3. English language—Grammar.   I. Society for the Promotion of Good
Grammar.   II. Title.
   PE1460.B77   2008
   428—dc22   2008018129

First Edition: October 2008

1   3   5   7   9   10   8   6   4   2

To Adam, Lucy, and Alice.
And to Steve Higgins, who would have liked this.

bcdef ghi jklm

opqrstuvwx

z123456789

!@#$%abc

fghijklmno

rstuvwxyz1

4567890!@

%^&.*()?."

Contents

Preface

It was the fall of 2004 when I founded the Society for the Promotion of Good Grammar after writing a column about secret societies for the online encyclopedia Encarta. The research astonished me. If you believe the reports, these secret societies run the free world and have for ages. It is true that some of their initiation rituals are unpleasant—unless you happen to be the sort who likes lying naked in a coffin, in which case, you might be reading the wrong book.

Macabre nudity aside, it seemed to me that running the free world would make a swell ambition. No longer would friends and family titter behind their hands when I mentioned that I'd studied English and classical studies in college. And, once I was in charge, I could do all sorts of good. For starters, I would see to it that no one would have to lie in a coffin without benefit of even undergarments. I needed only to figure out a platform: I knew what I wouldn't lie down for, but what would I stand for?

This led me back to the topic that has received the most reader interest in the eight years I've written for Encarta: grammar.

Every time I've discussed grammar or language in my

educational humor column, I've received hundreds of e-mail messages from people relieved to have someone defend correct writing and speech. While it is true that a movie column I wrote for MSN Movies titled "Nude Scenes I'd Rather Not See" ultimately generated more traffic, it's refreshing to note that good grammar takes a close second to bare skin.

To further the influence of my fledgling secret society, I built the SPOGG Web site anonymously, posting regular blog entries about grammar errors committed by celebrities, politicians, companies, and other power brokers. I also started writing stern letters to these high-profile offenders, as well as to Her Majesty the Queen, just to see what she thought had become of her English. (I believe she is not amused.)

This formed the heart of SPOGG's work: standing up for clean, correct, well-punctuated English. We're not the Society for the Promotion of Perfect Grammar, for several reasons. First, it would make a terrible acronym. Second, I am far too prone to errors despite my best intentions, and I'd lose my membership quickly. Third, perfect grammar is impossible to achieve in an ever-shifting sea of rules. And finally, there are cases when "good" is either good enough, or better than perfect.

What we seek above all else is clarity, for ourselves, and for the people we're communicating with.* Who knows how many of the world's huge problems could be solved if we had a little more of that?

As this book proves, we did eventually abandon the idea of

---

* It's fine in most cases to end a sentence with a preposition. If you must, skip ahead to chapter 10 to read all about it.

keeping the Society for the Promotion of Good Grammar a secret. Once the queen knew, it was going to be everywhere, anyway. She's *so* not mum. This public venture has no doubt forfeited our ability to rule the world clutching a red pen in our iron fists, but it's been altogether too enjoyable to meet thousands of like-minded people who've joined since we first organized.

With that, we welcome you to SPOGG. Feel free to clip this card and carry it with you always. You never know when you'll have to use it for the good of humankind.

This card certifies that

_____

is a member in good standing of

**The Society for the Promotion
of Good Grammar**

www.spogg.org

Membership is null and void if bearer uses myself instead of me.

Grammar for Spammers and Pop Stars

**The Society for the Promotion
of Good Grammar**

Dear Noah R. Estrada:

You accidentally sent us an e-mail meant for a Mr. Bret U. Sandoval. Ordinarily, we'd ignore this sort of thing, but we were so concerned for your grammar, we wanted to contact you so that you could clean things up a bit. Your mail read as follows:

> HAVE YOU EVER HEARD THIS, "GOD! YOUR PENI-5 IS REALLY TINY"?
>
> DIDN'T YOU FEEL, STUPID?
>
> DON'T LET THEM CHOOSE SEXUAL TOYS BUT NOT YOU! MEGADIK WILL MAKE YOU A REAL MAN ! YOU JUST HAVE TO TRUST THIS EXCELLENT PREPERATION!

We're not sure what a peni-5 is. Is that some sort of new currency? A poor cousin of the euro? If so, we agree; it would be annoying to have a small peni-5. The regular-sized ones are already hard enough to retrieve from gutters.

In any case, we wanted to let you know you might have inadvertently insulted Mr. Sandoval when you wrote, "Didn't you feel, stupid?"

We believe you meant to say, "Didn't you feel stupid?" The difference, of course, is that the first sentence calls him stupid, while the second empathizes with him for feeling that way because of his poor, tiny peni-5.

For all we know, Mr. Bret U. Sandoval might be the kind of guy who likes a little verbal spanking. We suspect, though, that you'd have more luck in general if you were kind to your customers in your correspondence.

In any case, good luck with Megadik. Whatever the effect of this preparation (that's the correct spelling, by the way), we're confident it's every bit as high quality as your e-mail advertising it.

Sincerely,

The Society for the Promotion of Good Grammar

P.S. There is no need to put a space before an exclamation point. Your penultimate sentence should read simply, "Megadik will make you a real man!"

If the state of language in popular culture is any indication, we're in trouble. As we write, *Billboard*'s list of top-selling albums contains two serious spelling errors: *Underground Kingz* by UGK, and *Dutchess* by Fergie. These aren't just bad;

they're royally bad. And it's not just musicians assaulting the language, either. We don't believe there has ever been a time when so many of society's rich and powerful have risen to their positions without first mastering the language of the land. Nor has there been a time when careful and correct use of the language—something that can only be learned by reading well, listening carefully, and sharpening skills—was routinely disdained as a vile act of the untrustworthy "elite."

Somehow the powers that be have decided to wage a costly and unnecessary war on the mother tongue. Someone in Los Angeles has decided that movie titles sound funnier with incorrect grammar, and that pop stars will have more credibility if they spell and punctuate as they please. Someone in New York has decided that "kids" and other plurals will sell more products when they're spelled with a terminal z. Someone in Washington, D.C., has decided that people who regularly bungle language can be called "plainspoken," when the truth is that people who actually speak plainly are the language masters, so skilled that their meaning is transparent without the use of long words, misleading jargon, or convoluted clauses.

This sort of mastery doesn't come without effort. Why do we allow this to be disparaged? If you wouldn't trust your hair to a stylist who hadn't mastered the craft, then why should you trust your cultural legacy to so-called artists who can't write songs, your money to marketers who butcher words, and your political future to any leader who hasn't mastered the ability to shape and convey his or her ideas?

It is time for those of us who love and respect our language to take it back. Clear, grammatical communication is society's foundation. It is what helps us understand and be understood.

If we let that bedrock crumble from neglect, or if we actively chip away at it in a misguided fit of anti-intellectualism, then we run the risk of watching the world around us collapse.

This is a dramatic picture, to be sure. But consider the difference in meaning a single comma gives these two simple sentences:

"Let's eat, children," is something a kind mother might say before offering a nutritious meal to her beloved offspring.

"Let's eat children" is something else entirely. And while the likes of Hannibal Lecter might like to eat the delicate flesh of babies, the rest of us—in the immortal and grammatical words of Bartleby the Scrivener—would prefer not to.

Knowing how punctuation and sentence structure can give collections of words the power to communicate complicated ideas is a good thing. We can, for example, let others know we merely intend to feed our children, and not eat them. Likewise, it's also good to know the meaning of individual words. Pajamas marked "INFLAMMABLE" are not flame-resistant; rather, they are liable to blaze up if exposed to extreme heat. It would be a shame, really, to resist eating your children only to lose them in an unintended bedroom barbecue.

These are unlikely misunderstandings, but that doesn't mean there are no risks to sloppy English. If you don't speak or write well, others are likely to assume you are stupid, uneducated, or both. Never mind that many of today's most powerful people have no grip on their grammar. If you're not a pop star or the president of the United States, you don't necessarily get a free ride on the language bus. We know of an otherwise lovely man who was not hired to be an editor because of a spelling goof on his Web site. During the interview, the hir-

ing manager was happy to overlook the large wad of spinach th͟
candidate had stored in his teeth. The spelling error, however,
sealed his fate.

What's more, the price can go beyond the mere professional. One woman we know—a ravishing expert in sexology
who has had exotic and erotic affairs around the globe—will
not date men whose personal ads contain errors. The errors in
typing, if they are so innocent, are costing these men certain
experiences we will not describe here, but that can be imag-
ined by those with even modest creative gifts. Bad grammar
can either screw you or leave you unscrewed. The Society for
the Promotion of Good Grammar refuses to take this lying
down.

Bad grammar is a particular irritant in two places: our
e-mail in-boxes and our ears. Try to go shopping without hearing the ubiquitous undulations of pop music. It's difficult, if not
impossible. Inevitably, the most embarrassing of those shopping songs take root as "earworms," a word translated from
German and thrust into popular usage by University of Cincin-
nati marketing professor James Kellaris. Synonyms include
"repetunitis" and "melodymania."

The danger, grammatically speaking, occurs when an ear-
worm infected with bad grammar dwells not just in your ear,
but in your mind. For even a seasoned speaker, it could blunt
your ability to know the difference between good grammar
and bad. And for vulnerable teens still struggling to use "I"
and "me" correctly, it could deafen their ears to the difference
between correct and incorrect speech.

While e-mail spam is far less likely to tattoo our minds, it is
still a huge problem. Some fifty-five billion pieces of unsolicited

t daily; this is about eight per man, woman, and
n the planet. And it's not just that the e-mail gener-
nlarge body parts half its recipients do not even
.... that the vast majority of this junk mail is hideously
ungrammatical. It's an affront to the eyes of anyone with any
sense. Worse, you can't write back and correct the grammar, lest
you want to confirm your e-mail address is a valid spam target.
It's the virtual equivalent of dog poop left on your lawn in the
cover of night. There's no stuffing it back from which place it
came. You must dispose of it daily, and it stinks.

This is why we have created two fantasy programs: grammar rehab for pop singers, and grammar court for spammers.
They're dreams today; may they someday come true.

GRAMMAR REHAB FOR THE RICH AND FAMOUS

TIMBERLAKE CLEANS UP AT "EDIT"

Manager: Star "Exhausted," Full Recovery Expected

(LOS ANGELES) Pop star Justin Timberlake today checked himself in for a
three-month stint at Each Day I Try, a glamorous Los Angeles center for
celebrities who've fallen off the grammar wagon.

Timberlake's people issued a statement that said the star "was ex-
hausted from the constant subject-verb disagreements in his lyrics. We
ask that his fans respect his privacy and dignity during this difficult time.
EDIT is a top-notch facility, and we expect him to be in perfect shape, both
grammatically and musically, after his treatment is complete."

On his MySpace page this message appeared briefly for his fans: "I
just want 2 be grammatically correct. I have a long way 2 go. Keep me in
UR thoughts."

The personal message was removed after only a few hours, and re-placed with the following: "We're keeping Justin away from the keyboard for his own good. Please keep him in ~~UR~~ ~~you're~~ your prayers."

(From Justin Timberlake's EDIT diary)

Dear Diary,

This is what I learned today from my grammar therapist: Any man who can dance like I can without losing his pimp hat *can* conjugate a verb. So I corrected the lyrics of "What Goes Around."

When you cheated girl
My heart ~~bleeded~~ bled girl

Then I realized that I'd punked my rhyme! So I changed it:

When you cheated girl
My heart did bleed, girl

Peace out! Do you think people are going to start wondering why I write songs about my girlfriends cheating on me whenever I'm breaking up with them? Man, that would suck worse than the Backstreet Boys.

Justin

Dear Diary,

I totally get verbs now. They're like *me*. They just want to get along with their subjects, which makes them royalty, which makes me the Prince of Pop. Bite that, Michael Jackson! You'd better hide your glove because I AM COMING FOR IT!

I think I will write a love song to verbs. Me and them, I mean, they and I will never break up. I'm not saying we're going to get married or anything, so Ellen DeGeneres can hold off on buying her bridesmaid's tuxedo. But damn! Verbs are about the love between equals.

And this is how I meant to write that part of "FutureSex/LoveSounds" (I am pleased to say I already spelled "you" right this time around:

You can't stop baby
You can't stop once you've turned me on
And your enemy ~~are~~ **is** *your thoughts baby [Because "enemy" is the*
subject of the sentence, not "thoughts"!]
So just let 'em go [Oops, missed that apostrophe first time around.
Good thing I put it in here.]

Peace out,
Justin

Dear Diary,

Today my therapist and I had the most interesting discussion. I had been reviewing the lyrics to "Like a Rolling Stone," which I thought was probably a Mick Jagger song, but turns out to have been written by this totally tight geezer named Bob Dylan.

I had some questions about his grammar. For example, he says, "When you got nothing, you got nothing to lose."

"Shouldn't that be 'you've got'?" I asked my therapist.

Her eyes got wet, like maybe a piece of dust landed in them or something. And she said, "Oh, Justin. That's where the artistry of the song comes in. While it technically would be correct to use the present-perfect tense, to indicate an action that began in the past and leads up to and includes the present, Dylan is increasing the folksy feel of his song by playing a bit with his verb tenses."

"How do you know he didn't just screw it up?" I asked.

"Just look at the rest of the lyrics of the song," she said.

You used to be so amused
At Napoleon in rags
And the language that he used
Go to him now, he calls you, you can't refuse
When you got nothing, you got nothing to lose

"Do you think anyone who'd craft an image about Napoleon in rags wouldn't know how to conjugate a verb?"

"Conjugate," I asked. "Is that the sort of visit you get in prison?"

"No," she said. "Not even close. Though many people derive similar pleasure from good grammar."

Then she slid something she'd written about verbs over to me [see "Things That Make Us Tense," page 167]. I read it. And I realized I could sing about so much more than I've been singing about if I just used more WORDS. I had no idea that words could actually do anything besides give my mouth something to do when I shake my groove thing.

I feel like a whole new man.

Xoxo,

Justin

TIMBERLAKE LEAVES REHAB, TELLS OF NEWFOUND "CREATIVE POWER"

(LOS ANGELES) Pop star Justin Timberlake today checked out of the high-profile Each Day I Try grammar rehab clinic.

"I have made a full recovery," Timberlake said to a throng of screaming teenage fans. He read from a prepared statement:

"No more will I use unnecessary abbreviations. I will ensure my subjects and verbs agree with each other. And I will use conventional word order and considered vocabulary wherever possible in my future songs.

"I just wish every artist knew how it felt to use the tools of language," he said. "I feel so much more creative power. I might even try to use actual metaphors in my songwriting now, so that I can sing about more topics than just wanting to go skin to skin with the ladyfolk."

Then Timberlake's manager jerked the microphone from his hands, while young Timberlake fans screamed and wept at the notion of more complicated songs.

"It's going to be a lengthy recovery period," Timberlake's manager said. "But don't think that good grammar will make him any less of a futuresex lovestallion.

"And you can quote me on that."

PSYCHIC CLAIMS TO HAVE MADE CONTACT WITH THE GHOST OF JIM MORRISON

(LOS ANGELES) Noted psychic Ivana Predict held a press conference today where she claimed to have spoken with the ghost of Doors lead singer Jim Morrison.

"He told me he wanted to make an apology," she said. "And it wasn't for wearing unwashed leather pants.

"His apology," she said, "was for singing the following lyric repeatedly: "I'm gonna love you 'til the stars fall from the sky / For you and I."

Predict continued: "Jim Morrison has been in Limbo since his death, but because the Pope just officially shut the place down, Mr. Morrison is being evicted. God told him he'd get into heaven if he agreed to no longer say 'for you and I' just for the sake of a cheap rhyme."

A representative of the Society for the Promotion of Good Grammar officially accepted the apology, and sent the Morrison estate a coupon for 30 percent off leather cleaning at a reputable chain.

The Thesaurus Awards

*

Not all musicians, of course, are guilty of grinding our language into a useless paste.

SPOGG hereby presents Thesaurus Awards to Michael Flanders and Donald Swann, Chuck Berry, and Arthur Hamilton.

The antepenultimate award goes to Flanders and Swann, who managed to work "antepenultimate"—which means third-to-last—into "Have Some Madeira, M'Dear."

> Then there flashed through her head what her mother
>   once said
> With her **antepenultimate** breath:
> "Oh my child, should you look on the wine when 'tis red,
> Be prepared for a fate worse than death!"
> She let go her glass with a shrill little cry.
> Crash, tinkle! It fell to the floor.
> When he asked "What in heaven . . . ?" she made no
>   reply,
> Up her mind and a dash for the door.

The penultimate award goes to Berry for incorporating "vestibule" (an entry or reception room) into "My Ding-a-Ling":

> And then mother took me to grammar school
> But I stopped off in the **vestibule**

> *Every time that bell would ring*
> *Catch me playin' with my ding a ling.*

The ultimate award, for use of non-plebeian language, goes to Arthur Hamilton, who wrote "Cry Me a River," which makes us cry tears of joy:

> *You told me love was too **plebeian**,*
> *Told me you were through with me an'*
> *Now you say you love me, well just to prove you do,*
> *Come on and cry me a river, cry me a river,*
> *I cried a river over you.*

SPAM POLICE: YOU'RE UNDER ARREST!

There is much about e-mail spam that puzzles us. We get why spammers send it, of course. It's about the money. One notorious spammer whose last name appropriately enough was "Pitylak" made $3 to $7 for each sucker he managed to lure with his unsolicited online propositions. We utterly lack pity for the million-dollar fine he racked up. (He had to sell a house and a BMW to pay it off, the poor dear.)

What we don't get is why it's so difficult for spammers to send grammatically correct e-mail. We don't care if they're actually working out of converted bunkers in those crazy Eastern-bloc countries that keep changing their names, using online translators to churn out spooky English. No one should want to buy medication that will change the size of vulnerable body parts from people who can't spell "pill."

But apparently some people don't care where their fake medicine comes from, which is why we continue to get such offers, even at e-mail addresses we have never distributed to anyone for any reason. People, please stop this.

Meanwhile, the Society for the Promotion of Good Grammar, Spam Police Division, issues the following citations for crimes against language.

Case No. 1: A "Unique" Snow Job
The Evidence (an Actual E-mail):

YOU CAN NOW FOR THE FIRST TIME, OWN A BUSINESS IN YOUR AREA WITH THE MOST UNIQUE, INNOVATIVE PRODUCT IN AMERICA TODAY. WORK LESS A WEEK WITH THE POTENTIAL TO EARN $100,000 A YEAR. THERE IS NO SELLING AND NOT MLM. JOIN A MULTI-TRILLION DOLLAR MARKET.

The Charges: Improper use of commas, abuse of the word "unique," serial word-dropping, criminal capitalization, and overall nonsensicality.

The Verdict: Guilty.

The Sentence: To have this edited version of your own spam tattooed on your forehead. Imagine how embarrassed you'll be when people ask you what it means and you have to try to sell them on this nonsense in person.

~~You can now for the first time,~~ Own a **unique, innovative** business ~~in your area with the most unique, innovative product in~~

~~America today.~~ Work less a each week, with the potential to earn $100,000 a year. There is no selling, and **the opportunity is** not ~~MLM~~ **multilevel marketing**. Join a multitrillion-dollar market.

Case No. 2: Too Little, Too Soon
The Evidence (Again, an Actual Spam):

BUT NOW I CAN PENETRATE HARDLY AND GIVE THE PLEASURE TO EVERY WOMAN!

The Charge: Too much information, inadvertently delivered.

The Verdict: Guilty! We suspect this spammer meant to describe his penetrative gifts with a different adverb: "hard." Although it does not end in -*ly*, "hard" is, indeed, an adverb in this sense. "Hardly," on the other hand, means "barely." And though we cannot speak for all recipients of penetration, we suspect the nigh-imperceptible sort is not the typical path to pleasure. It's also possible the seller was using truth in advertising, which we generally applaud—but not when it's unsolicited.

The Sentence: To wear a "Mister Softee" T-shirt in public (and to hang out with the guy who sent us an e-mail with the inadvertently funny subject line: THE ONLY SOLUTION TO PENIS ENLARGMENT! [Sic]).

Case No. 3: Talking Like Latka Gravas on *Taxi*
The Evidence (Actual E-mail):

ANATRIM—THE UP-TO-THE-MOMENT AND MOST ENCHANTING LOSE FLESH PRODUCT IS NOW READILY AVAILABLE—AS TOLD ON BBC.

Do you retain all the situations when you said to yourself you would do anything for being saved from this fastly growing pounds of fat? Happily, now no major sacrifice is expected. With Anatrim, the ground-breaking pound-melting medley, you can get healthier life style and become really thinner. Have a look at what people write!

"I had weight problems since a boy. You can't even fancy how I abhorred being derided at school. I hated the weight and I abhorred **even** myself. After trying many different remedies I heard about Anatrim. This stuff literally pulled me out of this terrible nightmare! Many and many thanks to you, my friends."

—Mike Brown, Boston

"Do you know what? Anatrim preserved my marriage! I went into the circle, depression—more eating—just more depression. My wife was about to leave me as I was turning in overweight psycho. My friend showed me web site and I called for my pack of Anatrim at the same time. The result was excellent, my appetite came to normal level, I was often in a good mood, and, certainly, I went some belt holes back. And you see me, the bedroom became cool, too!"

—Luis

There is a lot of thanks left by delighted people taking Anatrim. Why don't you join the thousands and thousands of slim buyers and try this natural appetite-suppressing energy boosting product now!

Do not decline the preposition!

The Charges: We're throwing the book at them. Literally. And we don't care if it leaves marks. That's how much is wrong with this.

The Verdict: Guilty of crazy-talk and repetitiveness.

The Sentence: A *proposition* they cannot decline, namely, a sound lashing with Luis's belt, now that he's too "thinner" to wear it.

Case No. 4: This One Left Us Speechless

Statistically speaking, it was inevitable that one properly composed spam would penetrate the e-universe. Here is that lone correct junk mail, recorded for posterity. Note: We're still not interested in the product.

VIAGRA

IF YOU HAVE A PROBLEM GETTING OR KEEPING AN ERECTION, YOUR SEX LIFE CAN SUFFER. YOU SHOULD KNOW THAT YOU'RE NOT ALONE. IN FACT, MORE THAN HALF OF ALL MEN OVER 40 HAVE DIFFICULTIES GETTING OR MAINTAINING AN ERECTION.* THIS ISSUE, ALSO CALLED ERECTILE DYSFUNCTION, OCCURS WITH YOUNGER MEN AS WELL!

YOU SHOULD KNOW THERE IS SOMETHING YOU CAN DO ABOUT IT. JOIN THE MILLIONS OF MEN WHO HAVE ALREADY IMPROVED THEIR SEX LIVES WITH VIAGRA!

---

* Note: This is correct as "erection," and not "erections." Though men are plural, they still only want one each—or so we fervently hope.

abcdefghijklm
nopqrstuvwx
yz1234567890
!@#$%abcd
fghijklmnop
qrstuvwxyz12
34567890!@#
%^&*()?.".

2.

Vizzinis, Evil Twins, and Vampires

Scene: A man in black climbs a rope that dangles from top of the Cliffs of Insanity. The Sicilian scoundrel Vizzini severs the rope with a knife. . . .

VIZZINI: HE DIDN'T FALL? INCONCEIVABLE!

INIGO MONTOYA: You keep using that word. I do not think it means what you think it means.

Cut to Canada. More specifically, Toronto, where it appears to be inconceivable to the natives that their Maple Leafs [*sic*] might be skating about* in ungrammatical jerseys.

---

* About. In Canadian, this is pronounced somewhere between "a-boot" and "a-boat."

**The Society for the Promotion
of Good Grammar**

Lawrence M. Tanenbaum
Chairman of the Board,
Maple Leafs Sports & Entertainment
40 Bay St., Suite 400
Toronto, ON M5J 2X2

Dear Mr. Tanenbaum,

We are the Society for the Promotion of Good Grammar, and we are writing to object, in the strongest possible language, to the name of your team.

We have no wish to create an international incident. Furthermore, we are frightened by the prospect of angering large men who carry sticks and live in a country that doesn't use the death penalty as a deterrent. Also, did we mention that we wear glasses?

Enough skating around the point. We cannot, in good conscience, leave you and your fans to wear jerseys marked with the incorrect plural form of "leaf."

In case your elementary school teachers never told you, when you have more than one leaf, you must call them leaves. Leaves. It's not hard to pronounce. It rolls off the tongue more easily even than "leafs," especially if one happens to be missing one's front teeth for any reason.

Perhaps a fresh and grammatical start such as this would be just the thing to earn the Maple Leaves a playoff berth next year.

We'll be watching (from a safe distance, just in case).

Sincerely yours,

SPOGG

The fan club for the Maple Leafs [*sic*] responded—amused, but unmoved.

Dear Martha,

Actually you are wrong. While many have been concerned with ·the spelling of our team's name, it is actually grammatically correct. Webster's Dictionary recognizes "leafs" as a possible plural of the word "leaf",* but also grammatically speaking, the Toronto Maple Leaf Hockey Club is a proper noun and when pluralizing proper nouns, one does not change the root word, in this case "Leaf†".

Therefore, one Toronto Maple Leaf hockey player would be a Toronto Maple Leaf while two or more Toronto players would be Toronto Maple Leafs. This is similar to a situation created with a family with the

---

* Canada follows British rules of punctuation, which call for commas and the like to fall outside of the quotation marks.

† We confess: We prefer the British system! But when in America. . . .

surname Leaf. You would refer to the family as "the Leafs" rather than changing their last name to Leaves.

I enjoyed your humour*; thanks for your mail, and thanks for being a fan.

Oh, Canada . . .

Dear Maple Leafs [*sic*],

Alas, we must protest. "Leafs" is not the plural of "leaf." Reputable dictionaries recognize "leafs"† as a word, but that word refers to the process of turning pages or putting forth foliage. It is in no way a universally accepted plural of "leaf."

Other teams have figured this out. Even though the Memphis Grizzlies are from the American South, a region not known for its grammatical regularity, they had the good sense not to be the Grizzlys. Even there, one player is a Grizzly.

Some will argue that repeated irregular usage becomes regular. We say, you can eat with your feet, and your spouse might get used to it, but your fussy neigh-

---

* British spelling! Crazy Canadians. You, too, could have had your independence!
† It's true that *Merriam-Webster's Collegiate Dictionary*, 11th ed. recognizes "leafs" as a secondary variant plural from of "leaf." This is the same dictionary that called "woot" its Word of the Year in 2007. We shouldn't have to point this out, but it's *not even made entirely of letters*. To return to the point, though, we believe that most normal people would cringe at hearing "leafs" tumble from the mouth of anyone not wearing diapers.

bor is still going to think of you as the weirdo next door who literally has jam between his toes.

Go Maple Leaves!

Sincerely,

SPOGG

ARE WE FORKED?

Consider the lowly fork: an everyday object, a vast improvement over chopsticks, but also a potential source of confusion, embarrassment, paralysis, and even damnation. We have forks for salad, forks for shrimp, and forks for instrument tuning. We encounter forked tongues and forks in the road. Satan, in his guise as Old Scratch, occasionally threatens us with the business end of a pitchfork. Please, don't even get us started on the dastardly mutt that is the spork. How is a person ever to know which fork to choose?

Words are a bit like this, and English is lousy with them—more so than most other languages. People who've taken the time to count say there are nearly 172,000 words in active use, with quite a few retirees on the side. This doesn't include creative obscenities, or much less their garden-variety counterparts. To make matters worse, many of these words sound similar or *exactly the same*. Which witch? Whose who's? Is it oar? Or ore? Arrr!

Choosing the wrong word, whether it's the wrong plural form, a soundalike, or just a word that sounds similar to the one you meant to use, is embarrassing. Choosing a word that isn't even a word is worse. It could cause people to permanently "misunderestimate"* you. Unlike at a fancy dinner party at the White House, where you can watch the First Lady and copy her fork choices, you're pretty much on your own when it comes to language, unless someone is standing there, pressing a pitchfork into your rib cage while you're trying to type. (Get thee behind me, Satan!)

We like to think of these words in several categories. There are the evil twins, words that sound the same, but are spelled differently and mean totally different things. On television, you can always tell which one is the evil twin: he has the goatee. Words offer no such helpful hairs. Knowing there are evil twins afoot is half the battle, though. When you're not sure which to use, you can refer to a dictionary (or this book) for help.

Equally confounding are the fraternal twins. These are the Mary-Kate and Ashley Olsens of our language. How do you tell them apart? You know they're slightly different; one is small; the other, smaller. But which one likes to drink bathtub-sized lattes? Which one lost her boyfriend to the hotel heir-head? Again, a cheat sheet ensures—not insures—you make the right choice.

Similar to fraternal twins are frequently fouled-up phrases. These are a bit like misheard song lyrics. The Bruce Springsteen song does not say "wrapped up like a douche, in the middle of the night." It's "revved up like a deuce,† another runner in the night." But who, not knowing any better,

---

* A nonword President Bush has used many times, though he has taken to correcting himself when it pops out of his mouth.
† "Deuce" means many things: a card or die with two spots; a $2 bill; or a tie-breaking situation in a racket game. Here, though, it means a souped-up car.

hasn't sung loudly about after-hours feminine-hygiene products?

The last category—and by far the most shameful—is for made-up words. These are vampires of our language. They don't exist. But their legend grows with use until, in some cases, they make it in the dictionary as "nonstandard" words. Like vampires, these generally suck, "irregardless" of what their defenders claim.

VIZZINIS TEN WORDS THAT MIGHT NOT MEAN WHAT YOU THINK THEY MEAN

If you are pressed for time, or if you're really old and fear you don't have much time left, or if you merely have limited space in your brain, here are ten everyday words you must learn to use correctly, lest you find yourself matching wits with a Sicilian when death is on the line.*

accept: To take something that is offered; to acknowledge or come to terms with a fact.
The trick: "Accept" starts with A. This is the only grade you will accept from your grammar teacher.

except: A preposition that means excluding, or a conjunction that means unless.
The trick: "Exclude" starts with E. (And "unless" has an e in it.)

---

* If you didn't get that one, you need to go watch *The Princess Bride*. Chop chop!

illicit: Means illegal or unacceptable.
The trick: If you do something illicit, you will feel ill afterward.

elicit: To provoke a reaction or draw out something hidden.
The trick: "Elicit" starts with *E*. If you draw out a scary hidden thing, you might say, "Eee!" Likewise, provoking someone might elicit a similar sound.

its: A possessive, but for something that is neither male nor female.
The trick: His towels, her towels, its towels (for the neutered dog or mooching cousin).

it's: A contraction.
The trick: If you can replace the word with "it is," then you need the apostrophe.

principal: The leader of a school, a significant person, a primary investor in something. This can be an adjective or a noun.
The trick: If a principal is someone important, you want to be her *pal*.

principle: A basic assumption, ethical standard, or way of working. This works only as a noun, and is not synonymous with a person.
The trick: If it's not a person, then it's *not* your pal.

whose: A possessive pronoun.
The trick: Whose towels? His, hers, and its. Possessive pronouns need no apostrophes.

who's: A contraction for "who is."

The trick: This is just like "it's." If you can swap in "who is," then it's a contraction and you need the apostrophe.

The Society for the Promotion
of Good Grammar

Mr. David Hasselhoff

Huge Star

Hollywood (and Germany)

Dear Mr. Hasselhoff,

The Society for the Promotion of Good Grammar is writing to congratulate you. It's not everyone who sees his life turned into a musical.

In fact, we can't think of any other men who've experienced this besides *Jesus Christ, Superstar* and that *Phantom of the Opera* fellow. Jesus never talked to cars, and the Phantom quite simply could not have pulled off the red *Baywatch* trunks. So you're in a league of your own. Bravo, Mr. Hasselhoff. Bravo!

We do, however, have one small problem. You say the show includes a "heart-rendering set on my life and the mistakes I have made."

One of those mistakes, we believe, was using the phrase "heart-rendering." To "render" means "to purify fat, leaving small, crisp remains." Surely that's not what you think of your life and career, or what you'd like to do to your fans' hearts.

It is possible that we have failed to anticipate a cooking scene in your musical, perhaps one with a pair of cantaloupes symbolizing your *Baywatch* costar Pamela Anderson. If that is the case, we apologize and say, *bon appétit*; we like our cantaloupe with a dash of pepper.

More likely, though, you meant to say "heartrending." That means either causing anguish or arousing deep sympathy, either of which makes us eager to see the show (though we find ourselves oddly in the mood for a brunch with bacon and melon slices).

Yours very truly,

SPOGG

EVIL TWINS

Evil twins are words that sound alike, but are spelled differently, and mean different things. In the 1980s, Hollywood gave us a decade-appropriate movie about a pair of identical twin brothers named Mantel. (Note: "Mantel" itself is an evil twin. A mantel is where one hangs stockings. This should not be confused with "mantle," which means coat.)

Played by the delightful Jeremy Irons, these twin brothers—gynecologists, even—are alike, but for one big difference: Twin A is more confident and therefore gets the first crack at the ladies. Then, once he tires of their companionship, he sends them along to the nebbish Twin B; the ladies are none the wiser. The plot thickens when a lovely actress comes in for her checkup and the shy brother gets to her first, both medically and emotionally.

Just as gynecologists have no business dating their patients, and identical twins have no business swapping their partners, nothing good will result from the accidental use of the wrong evil word-twin. In writing, the wrong word breaks the illusion of the story you're telling, leaving your readers to make unkind allusions about your literacy.

Like Jeremy Irons, though, these evil twins are good actors. It's easy to let them into your bed if you're not careful, and this momentary weakness can lead to a life spent wasted by the phone wondering why he doesn't call back. And so, the Society for the Promotion of Good Grammar offers this list, as a prophylactic against their unwanted advances into your prose. (It's all in a day's work for us pros.)

Allude/Elude

To "allude" is to mention indirectly, or to make a vague, hand-waving sort of reference. To "elude" is to escape (conveniently, "elude" and "escape" start with the letter *e*, so you will never confuse these words again).

Affect/Effect

"Affect" means to influence, stir emotions, infect with something, or harm. In psychiatric jargon, it also means manner. Unless you're in this line of work, the "affect" you use will always be a verb. "Effect," on the other hand, is a noun meaning result or impression. In formal contexts, "effect" can also mean to bring about, making it a verb to dust off, like crystal goblets, for fancy occasions. You can keep these two straight for the most part by remembering "affect," with an *a*, is an action word, or verb.

Allusion/Illusion

An "allusion" is an indirect reference. See "allude" if you've forgotten already. An "illusion" is something with a deceptive appearance, or it's a false idea. If something tricks you, you're going to feel *ill* when you find out the truth. That's how you can remember "illusion."

Altar/Alter

An "altar" is a raised ceremonial structure, where sheep, grooms, and other animals are sacrificed. To "alter" is to change, or in certain contexts, to castrate. It's easy to see how many could be altered after a trip to the altar. The way to remember the difference? "Alter" with an *e* is a verb. Change can make us all say, "Eeeek!"

Bare/Bear

One means to reveal; the other is a furry creature or a verb that means to carry. Do not say "bare with us" unless you are at a nudist colony.

Board/Bored

A "board" is flat piece of wood, or a surface for playing games. "Bored" means tired and impatient. It's an adjective. We sincerely hope you're not bored right now. But if you are, you have our permission to skip ahead to "whored."

Born/Borne

Babies are born; burdens are borne. You can remember the difference by noting that *e* at the end—it's a burden for borne to bear. (Note: children can be borne, too, as long as their mother is in the sentence doing the heavy lifting. *She had borne two children by the time she was thirty-five; the gray hairs soon followed.*)

Brake/Break

A "brake" slows down a machine or acts as a restraint. It's a noun. "Break," on the other hand, is a utility player. It has fifty-some meanings as a verb (including, in the Caribbean, what the French call "a little death"). Its primary meaning as a verb is to separate into pieces. As a noun, it means to take a brief or permanent vacation from a relationship, a distinction Ross failed to make clear when he and Rachel were "on a break."

Callous/Callus

No one wants a callus, and not many more people want to be callous. A "callus" is a patch of thickened skin. How unsavory! "Callous" is an adjective meaning hard-hearted. Think of the *o* in the middle of the word as a heart that's turned to stone; then you'll remember which word to use.

Capitol/Capital

"Capitol" with an *o* is a building for a law-making body (a noun). This is easy to remember because capitols so often contain circular buildings called rotundas. "Capital" with an *a* is used for all other meanings of the word: political power;

money for investing; serious (as in crime); uppercase letters; and the city where a government center is located. If there's no *o* or rotunda, it's the *a* version of "capital."

Carrot/Karat/Carat/Caret

A "carrot" is an orange vegetable that can protect your eyesight (really!). The equally important "karats" and "carats" refer to the measure of gold content in a metal alloy and the weight of the gems that can be set in said alloy. The most important type of identical twin, however, is the "caret." This proofreading mark indicates missing text, and forms the legs of the SPOGG "grammar avenger" logo.

Cite/Sight/Site

To "cite" is to quote, name, praise, or compel to appear in court. It's a verb. "Sight" is the ability to see, or something worth seeing, or an alignment device on a weapon (which, if used illegally, can cause one to be "cited" with a misdemeanor or worse). A "site" is a significant location—as in, the site of said misdemeanor (or SPOGG.org).

Compliment/Complement

A kind word or bit of praise is a "compliment." A "complement" *completes* something. Notice that "complements" and "complete" share their first six letters. This is a good way to remember which is which.

Demur/Demure

"Demur" is a verb that means to show reluctance; to object somewhat. "Demure" is an adjective that means looking or acting modest and shy. Think of that final *e* as a hand curled in front of the mouth, as shy ladies are wont to do in corny old cartoons.

Discreet/Discrete

"Discreet" means tactful, subtle, modest, or good at keeping secrets. "Discrete" means completely separate. Look at those *ee*'s in discrete, rendered *completely separate* by the *t*. That's the way to remember which is which.

Ensure/Insure

This is such a tricky pair—like a pair of legs (bear with us here). To "ensure" means to make something certain. "Insure" means to cover something with insurance or protect against risk. Use the I-word if it has to do with your car, homeowner's, rental, dental, medical, life, pet, or leg insurance. Don't scoff; Mariah Carey insured hers for $1 billion; if they're damaged beyond repair, she can triple her net worth, ensuring a highfalutin (if not high-kicking) lifestyle for the rest of her days.

Flair/Flare

A "flair" is a talent or sort of elegance. "Flares" are sudden flashes of flame, or pants with very wide legs. (Totally coincidentally, both types of flares represent a cry for help.)

Forego/Forgo

"Forego" means to come before something. To "forgo" means to go without something—as in the letter *e* that the other kind of forego got. You can spell the second kind of forego with the *e*, but this isn't the preferred way to do it.

Forward/Foreword

The core of the word "forward" means toward the front, either in placement or direction. "Forewords" are the forward part of books. You can remember this because fore*words* contain words.

Hay/Hey

"Hay" is cut grass that has been dried. It's also slang for a small amount of money (but for this, we prefer "cheddar"). "Hay" is also what one of our nephews types when he wants to get our attention in instant messenger. "Hey" is what he means to type.

Hoard/Horde/Whored

To "hoard" is to sock away a supply of something (say, nuts, or gemstones). A "horde" is a large group of people or animals. "Whored" is to have worked as or regularly visited a prostitute. One would hope that anyone who has whored has managed to hoard some money for a legal defense fund, which will be necessary when the hordes of police come bearing handcuffs.

Led/Lead

"Led" is the past tense of the verb "lead." "Lead" is a heavy metal. "Led" Zeppelin is not a heavy metal band, which is why they're not to be chastised for spelling it thus.

Metal/Mettle/Meddle/Medal

In addition to being a type of music, "metal" is a chemical element that is usually solid, shiny, and quick to heat. "Mettle" is temperament or strength of character. To "meddle" is to mess with or interfere. A "medal" is what you win in a competition after your mettle has been tested, provided no one meddles with your backswing. Medals are usually made of metal.

Past/Passed

"Past" is an adjective that means elapsed. Working as a preposition, it can also describe movement. You go past a person, place, or thing, for example. "Passed" is a verb that means you've moved past something, or overtaken it.

Peak/Pique/Peek

The "peak" is a noun meaning the highest point, or a verb that means to reach the highest point.

"Pique" means either a bad mood, or to put someone in a bad mood. It can also mean to arouse interest. It might arouse your interest to know we used to get in a bad mood trying to remember how to spell "pique." Then again, it might not. Sorry!

"Peek," meanwhile, is a quick look, or to look quickly. Don't those double *e*'s look like shifty little eyes?

Pore/Pour

A "pore" is a tiny opening in skin, plants, or rocks. It also means to study, concentrate, or reflect on something. To "pour" is to make something flow. Note the *ou* in both "pour" and "you." May I pour you a drink?

Shudder/Shutter

"Shudder" means to shiver violently, or to tremble. "Shutter" is a door or window cover; it also means to close. (Oh, and cameras have shutters, but it's kind of complicated explaining how they work.) We once saw a political candidate write, "I shutter to think. . . ." This made us shudder. His campaign, by the way, was shuttered shortly thereafter.

Than/Then
"Than" follows an adjective or adverb that's comparing one thing to another. "Then" indicates a time in the past or future.

They're/There/Their
"They're" is a contraction for "they are." That apostrophe is a clue to you that letters have been squeezed out of a two-word pileup. "There" is usually an adverb, and its central meaning indicates a place. It can also be an interjection, as in, "There!" Or a pronoun, introducing a sentence or limerick. *There once was a man from Nantucket.* "Their" is an adjective or possessive pronoun that means belonging to them.

To/Too/Two
"To" is a useful little word that indicates where you are, or where you're headed. It can indicate a range (from A to B), a recipient (to me), and the infinitive (to be, or not to be). "Too" means in addition to (it's an *o* in addition to the original *to*). It also means "more than you'd want." As in, too cold, too hungry, or too wet behind the ears. "Two" is the number it takes to tango. The *w* in "two" looks to us a bit like an aerial view of two people tangoing.

Vice/Vise
A bad habit or character flaw is a "vice." Lest you think this means the vice president is necessarily flawed, the word

also means in place of. As in, in place of the president should he have a heart attack on the golf course. A "vise," on the other hand, is a clamp. Even off the other hand, it's a vise. Note: We do not recommend that you put a vise on your hand.

Weather/Whether

The "weather" is what you talk about at dull parties, an especially painful subject in places like Arizona, where it's always the same. "Whether" is a conjunction that introduces alternatives or indirect questions—whether you like it or not.

FRATERNAL TWINS

In the human context, fraternal twins often look similar and sound similar, and yet, they're not the same. Often the only way you can tell them apart is if they're standing side by side, and with any luck, wearing bowling shirts helpfully embroidered with their names.

Generally speaking, the universe is not this kind. In fact, more often than not, fraternal twins don't bowl, and their parents further confused matters by giving them names that started with the same letters. We never could tell the difference between Dear Abby and Ann Landers. Perhaps not coincidentally, these women spent their adult lives feuding (even as they counseled other feuding families).

Meanwhile, the same thing happens with words. Take "stanch" and "staunch." The Old French word *estanchier* is great-grandmother to them both. But they're not the same (even though some wanton sorts would like them to be). Over the years, "stanch" has most often been used as a verb that means to stem the flow. "Staunch," meanwhile, means steadfast and loyal.

Other commonly confused words are not even blood relatives. They just look alike, separated at birth as were that Ollie North fellow and the flying monkeys from *The Wizard of Oz*. We could tell you an anecdote about the time a former coworker kept describing the stories she was telling as "antidotes," but that would probably be boring. The antidote to that, of course, would be simply to provide a list of the fraternal twins, and tips for keeping them straight.

All Ready/Already

"All ready" means totally prepared. You emphasize the "all" when you say it. "Already" means by now; you punch the "red" when you pronounce it. Get all ready, already!

Adverse/Averse

"Adverse" effects are unpleasant ones. "Averse" means opposed to. One should be averse to experiencing the adverse effects of an inexpensive sushi lunch.

Anecdote/Antidote

An "anecdote" is a short story. An "antidote" is a remedy, or something that counteracts poison.

Assume/Presume

To "assume" means to suppose something is true without confirming it. To "presume" means, among other things, to believe something is true. They're so close! And yet, they're not entirely synonymous. To assume suggests a belief that's going to stay around for a while. To presume connotes a starting belief that might be changed with more evidence. It's "presumed innocent," not assumed. There's also that helpful Benny Hill joke: To assume is to make an ASS out of U and ME.

Assure/Ensure/Insure

In our evil twins section, we talked about the differences between "ensure" and "insure." We keep this straight by thinking fondly of our insurance bill. Paying this is what ensures we'll be protected from the petty thieves and insane arsonists of the world. "Assure" sounds similar, but it has a meaning all its own. It means to guarantee something will happen, or to convince someone of something. We remember this word by noting its first three letters: *ass*. As in, only an ass could be assured he could do without insurance; we live in a world that requires significant amounts of it to protect us from petty thieves and insane arsonists.

Beside/Besides

"Beside" is a preposition, and it means next to. "Besides" is an adverb that means more, or in addition to. The *s* gives it more letters, in addition to the root word, beside.

Bimonthly/Semimonthly

Is it too scandalous to say we remember "bimonthly" by thinking of bisexual? Two ways, every two months. Okay, too scandalous. So think seminude instead. That's half dressed, for every half month.

Censor/Censure

To "censor" is to suppress or remove. To "censure" is to criticize severely. The Society for the Promotion of Good Grammar believes in censuring censors—unless it's done in the name of clean, clear language.

Closer/Closure/Cloture

A "closer" is a relief pitcher, or someone who closes something. A "closure" is a permanent end to a business, the act of closing something, or that satisfied feeling you get after you see a former flame's mink farm was shut down after the animals staged a bloody rebellion. (There are other meanings specific to politics, mathematics, phonetics, and geology; most people won't need to know these.) "Cloture," meanwhile, is a term senators use when they want to end a debate and vote on a matter. It's pronounced KLOH-cher.

Concur/Agree

Both mean to agree, but to "concur" has a more specific power and implies to agree, but not necessarily for the same reasons. This is why judges sometimes write concurring opinions.

Continuous/Continual

"Continuous" means uninterrupted. "Continual" means frequently. Our two-year-old, whose chatter is continuous, interrupts us continually.

Convince/Persuade

"Persuade" and "convince" are two words that can almost be used interchangeably, not unlike identical twin gynecologist brothers. But there is a wee difference. When you're persuading someone, you're not necessarily going to convince him or her. "Persuade"'s original meaning was to urge strongly. To convince comes from the Latin *convincere*, which means to prove wrong. So if you want a word that's more definite, we hope we've convinced you which one to use.

Dissemble/Disassemble

To "dissemble" is to lie or mislead. To "disassemble" is to take something apart.

Disinterested/Uninterested

If you're "disinterested" in something, you're Switzerland. You're neutral. You're not invested in the outcome, though you will happily invest others' money in your massive banks. If you're "uninterested," you're bored—something that can't happen in Switzerland, with its banks, chocolates, towering mountains, and cuckoo clocks.

Emit/Omit

One "emits" (or gives off) odors. To maintain marital bliss, one "omits" from daily conversations the fact that one's spouse smells bad.

Farther/Further

Use "farther" when discussing things that can be measured, such as distance. Use "further" when it's a matter of degree. You drive farther; you discuss further.

Faze/Phase

A "phase" is a stage, whether of the moon, or of trying behavior in childhood. To "faze" is to fluster or disconcert. The full moon can faze you, as can the trying behavior of your children. Both, blessedly, are phases.

Flaunt/Flout

To "flaunt" is to show off. To "flout" is to ignore a law or convention. A flaunting flouter—let's say, a celebrity who made a show out of cutting in line at the bathroom—would be seriously irritating.

Historic/Historical/Histrionics

"Historic" and "historical" are spawn of the same noun, "history." But "historical" means something that merely happened in the past; "historic" means something historical that was also important. It's the difference between having a noteworthy ancestor, and having an ancestor who polished that person's boots. "Histrionics," meanwhile, are overdone emotions. We once heard the broadcaster/New Age musician John Tesh use "histrionics" when he meant "historic" during an Olympic ice-skating telecast. With figure skating, though, the word almost works.

Imply/Infer

To "imply" is to put meaning into something; to "infer" is to make a conclusion (or take meaning out of something).

Lend/Loan

Although some people insist "lend" is a verb and "loan" is a noun, reasonable people who wish no harm upon the English language have agreed that they're pretty much interchangeable—except in one context. When you help someone out, you lend him or her a hand. You don't loan it; chances are you wouldn't get it back.

Loath/Loathe

"Loath" means reluctant. "Loathe" is to hate. We should be loath to loathe; it causes forehead wrinkles.

Loose/Lose

"Loose," which rhymes with "goose," means wiggly or unfastened. "Lose," which rhymes with "shoes," is what you end up with when one of the *o*'s in loose becomes unfastened and rolls away.

Nauseous/Nauseated/Nauseating

If you're "nauseous," you make people sick. If you're "nauseated," other people have made you sick. Something "nauseating" is deeply disgusting.

Peaked/Peaked/Peeked/Piqued

If you've "peaked," you're past your prime. But if you're "peak*ed*" (where the *-ed* is pronounced as a separate syllable), then you're pale and sickly. If this happened because you "peeked" at something you shouldn't have seen, then you got what you deserved. (Your just "*deserts*," not "desserts"; those are for good boys and girls.) And if you're "piqued" at having received such deserts, you're feeling peeved.

Pore/Pour and Poor

"Pore" and "pour" are evil twins (see page 35 for their meanings). "Poor" is pronounced slightly differently. To be poor is to lack something, usually money. (People are sometimes "poor in spirit," among other things.)

Stanch/Staunch

"Stanch" means to stem the flow; "staunch" means steadfast or loyal. Although "staunch" can be used to stem the flow as well, the Society believes words are more powerful when their meanings are narrow. That way, you have a precise word with specific meaning when you need it. The word "nice," for example, has been used to mean ignorant, foolish, dainty, timid, slutty, or strange. Now, it's used to describe everything from neckties to the weather to teenage girls who don't put out. Like an expiring pair of panty hose, the word has been worn thin and flimsy. It would be . . . nice to stanch this tide before we lose another fine word.

Trough/Troth

Pigs (and other animals) eat from "troughs," which are containers or channels. A "troth" is a solemn vow, as in the one you make on your wedding day. Not that it's any of our business, but SPOGG hopes you never pledge your troth to a pig.

While/Wile

"While" means during, though one can "while away" hours if one chooses to spend time idly. A "wile," meanwhile, is a trick or ruse. For some reason, there are feminine wiles, but no one complains of masculine ones.

The Society for the Promotion of Good Grammar

U.S. Rep. Jay Inslee
Shoreline Center
18560 1st Ave., NE
Suite E-800
Shoreline, WA 98155-2150

Dear Congressman Inslee,

Greetings from the Society for the Promotion of Good Grammar!

And now for the bad news: Our members were listening to you on our local NPR affiliate when we heard something that positively pinched our ears. While explaining your position on illegal immigration, you said, "We need to have control over our borders to *staunch* this flow." (The italics are ours.)

We believe the word you meant to use was "stanch."

Although "stanch" and "staunch" share origins, and although some grammatically liberal types use them interchangeably, this is the equivalent of putting your socks on your hands and calling them mittens. It might be perfectly functional, but people who know better will look at you askance.

SPOGG recommends using "stanch" when you're in need of a verb that means to stop the flow. Then, when you find yourself in need of an adjective that means loyal and dependable, you will have a fresh supply of "staunch" at the ready.

Ultimately, this will keep your meaning clear, which, in politics these days, is all too rare.

Staunchly,

SPOGG

MALAPROPISMS AND MONDEGREENS

When the literary rascal Ramona Quimby heard the national anthem, she thought she'd learned a new word for lamp. It was "the dawnzer-lee light," after all. Hilarity ensued when she pressed the word "dawnzer" into service.

Mirth does not occur when a grown-up, particularly one with great political power, reaches into his box of words and pulls out the wrong one. For example, when a certain leader of the free world said, "You took an oath to defend our flag and our freedom, and you kept that oath *underseas* and under fire," SPOGG blanched and started researching real estate in Canada's maple leaf–lined streets.

There are special words for such things: "malapropisms"

and "mondegreens." "Malapropism" comes partly from the word "malapropos," coined in the 1600s to mean inappropriate, and even more from a character in a play written in 1775 by Richard Sheridan. The character—Mrs. Malaprop—said such things as "He's the very pineapple of politeness." Mondegreens, meanwhile, are misheard phrases. The word itself is one, coined by the author Sylvia Wright, who heard "Lady Mondegreen" instead of "laid him on the green."

Unless you aspire to be the pineapple of absurdity, here are some phrases worth learning, before you, too, are laid on (or under) the green.

By and large: Not "by in large" or "buy in large" (unless, of course, that is your size). This bit of sailor's parlance terms means all possible circumstances.

Could have: Not "could of." Ever. We saw this usage crop up repeatedly in a novel narrated by a boy who died a terrible death under a heavy slab of Sheetrock, a fate deserved by anyone who gets this one wrong.

Flesh it out: Not "flush it out." Unless, of course, you're talking about something in the toilet.

For all intents and purposes: Not "for all-intensive purposes."

Grin and bear it: Not "grin and bare it." Please! Put it away. No one wants to see that.

I'd just as soon: Not "I just assume."

Moot points: Not "mute points," unless you're talking with a mime.

Quote, unquote: Not "quote, end quote." You can quote us on that. (But please refrain from making the quote fingers.)

Safe-deposit box: Not "safety-deposit box."

Take it for granted: Not "take it for granite." P.S. Formica doesn't fool us.

Worst-case scenario: Not "worse-case." Note: A related phrase is historically rendered as "worse comes to worse." Modern ears hear the still logical "worse comes to worst." The second runner-up, "worst comes to worse," makes no sense.

MAKE THE PIE HIGHER

A poem by George W. Bush

Assembled by Richard Thompson of the Washington Post,
used with permission

I think we all agree, the past is over.
This is still a dangerous world.
It's a world of madmen and uncertainty
and potential mental losses.

Rarely is the question asked
Is our children learning?
Will the highways of the Internet become more few?
How many hands have I shaked?

They misunderestimate me.
I am a pitbull on the pantleg of opportunity.
I know that the human being and the fish can coexist.
Families is where our nation finds hope, where our wings take dream.

Put food on your family!
Knock down the tollbooth!

Vulcanize society!
Make the pie higher! Make the pie higher!

VAMPIRES

There are two kinds of language people in the world: the ones who believe language has firm rules that must be respected forever, and the ones who believe the rules are rewritten all the time by the people using the language. In other words, if it's spoken, it can't be wrong.

They're both right. They're also both totally wrong.

Language evolves, of course. It must make room to accommodate Homer Simpson's "d'oh," and the "bling bling" that is a rapper's delight. When such words move into the culture, sensible people don't say, "There goes the neighborhood." They bring over a plate of cookies and try to gain traction for their own neologism, "frathletic," which means muscular, boorish, yet popular, nonetheless. (Someday, *someday*, the nerd hopes, she will have one single, nonprofane word to describe the boys who made high school so unpleasant.)

But this doesn't mean any old thing goes. Language is also a bit like a planned community. When you live in a planned community, you just can't go jamming plastic flamingos and Confederate flags into your front lawn. It's against the rules—rules that make life more pleasant for us all. It keeps the place looking neat and orderly, it keeps us from making a spectacle of ourselves, and it beats the heck out of the jungle.

Nowhere is this truer than with word choice. There are certain words, widely used, that *simply aren't words*. Or not words of a respectable variety, at least. The dictionary might call them "nonstandard." This is not a compliment, nor should it be taken as an endorsement of their worth. There is a time and a place for nonstandard uses for everyday things, and that time and place is during a *MacGyver* rerun. Candy bars and paper clips make fine nonstandard weapons on prime-time television. But Mac-Gyvers have no place in your mouth, unless you're spitting them out with derision. *Irregardless! The bastard spawn of regardless and irrespective! It's redundant! Unnecessary! Blecch!*

These words are the vampires that sneak into language in the dark of night, rounding up defenseless converts for their dark and remorseless army, sucking the lifeblood from perfectly good words that deserve to go about their little lives. We must think of ourselves as replacements for the dearly missed *Buffy the Vampire Slayer*, sending these suckers back to their dusty origins.

Here are twenty words and expressions that need a firm and fatal introduction to Mr. Pointy, the vampire-killing stake.

Acrosst: Use "across."

All new: Use "new." TV networks promise "all new" episodes. With the exception of *Three's Company* and cheesy clip montages, have the networks ever given us "partly new" shows?

Alot: Use "a lot."

Anyways: Use "anyway."

A ways: Use "a way."

Conversate: "Converse."

Crème: A French word for cream. Not a color, nor a description for the filling inside a baked good. "Crème de la crème," which means cream of the cream, is a cliché. Avoid it.

Disorientated: Use "disoriented." Unless you're feeling woozy from eating disorientater-tots.

Expresso: Contains no x. Use "espresso" (or keep drinking your Nescafé).

Excetera: Also X-rated. Use "et cetera."

Gifted (when used as a verb): Here in America, in the twenty-first century, "gift" is a noun; "give" is a verb. Do not "gift us" with the opposite, as it smacks of marketing-speak.

Heighth: "Height."

Irregardless: Use "irrespective" or "regardless."

Lite: Let it be "light." Same goes for thru/through and wuz/was. (This one, to us, is really inexplicable—it doesn't even save any letters!)

Old-timer's disease (and arthuritis): Use "Alzheimer's" and "arthritis." (But try to avoid contracting either.)

Structurized: "Structure." (See "Dear Infusium," below.) Adding -*ize* to the end of a word is something that should be done with great care, lest you invite a vampire inside your home.

Supposably: Use "supposedly."

Volumptious: Use "voluptuous." It's curvy, not lumpy.

Wreckless: Use "reckless." Unless you're talking about your clean driving record.

The Society for the Promotion
of Good Grammar

Dear Infusium shampoo company,

The Society for the Promotion of Good Grammar applauds your attempts to rid the world of frizzy, unmanageable hair, but we are, at the same time, concerned with some of the language of your marketing campaign.

You claim your product "corrects, restores and *structurizes*" hair. (The italics are ours.) As you rightly recognize that the English language does not yet correctize or restorize, it does not yet structurize either. It structures, just as Infusium—if it lives up to the language of your advertisements—structures limp or otherwise unruly hair.

It is not as though SPOGG is opposed to coining new words when clear and lively expression demands them. We like how Infusium makes it sound as though hair will be infused with some space-age, frizz-taming magic. When our language already has words that perform the task at hand, however, we believe those are the words that should be employed, instead of mutant offspring that sound, to our ears, as split ends might appear to your own eyes.

SPOGG is grateful for the time you took in reading this letter, and would feel a collective thrill if you would be so good as to correct your advertisement.

Sincerely yours,

SPOGG

abcdefghijklm
nopqrstuvwx
yz123456789
0!@#$%abcd
efghijklmnop
qrstuvwxyz12
34567890!@#
%^&*()?".:

3.

You Put a Spell on Me

BE ADEQUITE.

—LINDSAY LOHAN

I don't see any use in having a uniform and arbitrary way of spelling words. We might as well make all clothes alike and cook all dishes alike. Sameness is tiresome; variety is pleasing. I have a correspondent whose letters are always a refreshment to me, there is such a breezy unfettered originality about his orthography. He always spells Kow with a large K. Now that is just as good as to spell it with a small one. It is better. It gives the imagination a broader field, a wider scope. It suggests to the mind a grand, vague, impressive new kind of a cow.

—MARK TWAIN

CONFIDENTIAL TO FORMER CONGRESSMAN MARK FOLEY,
R-Florida
RE: Grammar and spelling in erotic text messages
sent to teenagers
FROM: The Society for the Promotion of Good
Grammar

Dear Rep. Foley:

In the event you once again find yourself leading the people of the great state of Florida, and resuming control over such things as the House Caucus on Missing and Exploited Children, the Society for the Promotion of Good Grammar would like to provide you with some confidential spelling and grammar advice.

We have taken the liberty, as it were, to correct some of the many errors that appeared in instant messages you exchanged with one of your pages. We believe this information will come in handy the next time you discuss political matters with a teenager while he's waiting for his mom to serve supper.

1. It's "keep scrounging," not "kep scrounging."

2. "Boo" is spelled with two *o*'s.

3. Pensacola, the oldest city in the state you represent, is spelled with an *a* in the middle, not an *e*.

4. "How my favorite young stud doing" is not grammatical; it should be "How's my favorite young stud doing?" Or, "How is my favorite young stud doing?"

5. The *h* comes before the *a* in "that's good." Also, "that's" requires an apostrophe. If we didn't know better, we'd think you were typing with one hand.

6. You are missing apostrophes in "dont ruin my mental picture" and "youll be way hot then."

7. It's "go do your thing," not "oyur thing."

8. "Hand job" has only one *a*.

9. It's "you're getting horny," not "your."

10. It should be "I am never too busy," not "to" busy.

11. Oops! Another missing apostrophe in "That's a good number."

12. The phrase is "sounds interesting," not "sound inetersting."

13. When you say "well I have aa totally stiff wood now," you need a comma separating "well" from the rest of the sentence. Also, the article is unnecessary. "Well, I have totally stiff wood now."

14. It's "that would hurt," not "taht would hurt."

15. It's "spurting," not "spirting."

16. Missing apostrophe alert: it's "that's wild," not "thats wild."

17. "What you wearing" is missing a verb and punctuation. It should be "What are you wearing?"

18. The word is not spelled "buldge." It's "bulge."

19. "One-eyed snake" needs a hyphen.

20. We presume you mean "you're hard," not "your hard."

21. "Cool hope se didnt see any thing" contains numerous errors. The sentence should read, "Cool—hope she didn't see anything."

Should you have any further need for our assistance, please don't hesitate to contact us.

Sincerely,

SPOGG

SPELLING: NOT BIG FOR CAVEMEN

Cavemen probably could have used shampoo. Deodorant? Bring it. Detangling conditioner? A fine luxury. Dictionaries, alas, would have been another story. Yes, a thick dictionary could be tossed on a fire pit and used to lend a provocative smokiness to the mastodon chops sizzling in the flames. Otherwise, though, it would be useless. Cavemen—the ancestors of us all—didn't need to spell.

Experts in such things believe humans didn't even have written language until about 3,500 years ago. In contrast, our prehuman ancestors knew how to hunt, make fire, and fashion clothing for a far longer period—350,000 years. And as long as 35,000 years ago, our human ancestors were practicing religion and making art, and maybe even mixing the two.

Yes, writing would someday come. But it was hardly the most necessary thing to their survival and our own existence on this planet. Written language—let alone the properly spelled sort—offered no protection against thunderstorms, deadly bacterial infections, or saber-toothed beasts. If you were to give a caveman a piece of chalk, he wouldn't write "TIGERS SUCK" or even "TIGER'S SUK." He'd be far more likely to draw tigers, or, on happy days, dancing kows (making graphic novels our oldest form of literature). Such artistic ability may have served as an aphrodisiac, along with good health, robust muscles, and the sort of intelligence that led to the creation of the wheel.

In any case, it's certain that no meaningful numbers of children were conceived following well-spelled notes of woo. Those things weren't to come for millennia. Given what went into shaping and perpetuating the human race, it's not a big surprise that the ability to spell isn't part of our genetic makeup. (In case you do not believe in evolution: Experts say the Bible itself is riddled with errors. We could blame those on the humans who copied the good book, but that introduces all sorts of uncomfortable issues about the infallibly divine nature of its contents, doesn't it? In any case, we have ample evidence that God was excellent at geography and biology. He could have been a terrible speller and no one would have held back his diploma.)

This news might soothe those of us who suffer when putting words to paper. But it doesn't mean you can spell badly and not endure the consequences. Consider the sad case of former vice president Dan Quayle.

"You're close," he told the twelve-year-old boy who had already spelled "potato" correctly on the blackboard. "You left a little something off," Quayle said. "The *e* on the end."

Alas for Mr. Vice President, there is no *e* on the end of "potato." It requires the company of other potatoes to earn that final vowel.

Later, Quayle wrote in his memoir: "It was more than a gaffe. It was a 'defining moment' of the worst imaginable kind. I can't overstate how discouraging and exasperating the whole event was."

Though he blamed faulty cue cards for the errant *e*, this defining moment sealed his reputation as a boob, and perhaps one with a weak imagination, at that. We can imagine worse moments than misspelling "potato," especially when you're vice president during the first Gulf War. This was, after all, a matter of mortality, not mere mortification. Even so, we do understand his dismay. It is perhaps telling that while George H. W. Bush's face was carved in marble and displayed in the vice-presidential bust collection a mere two years after he concluded his term as veep, it took more than a decade for Quayle's likeness to be similarly enshrined. Talk about a career bust.

We lesser mortals have those to look forward to if we misspell on the job, or on our résumés. If we spell badly in our personal ads, we will not have opportunities to procreate. Criminals have been convicted in part because of idiosyncratic spelling tics. And the *Journal of Learning Disabilities* has even linked spelling problems with suicide.

The sad part is that while good spelling isn't wired into our genes, bad spelling probably *is* genetic. Scottish researchers recently conducted a twenty-year study that identified thirteen genes linked to your ability to process letters and numbers. If you don't have the lucky sequence, you're going to need help with your spelling, regardless of how bright you are.

It all seems terribly unfair that we're saddled with a language that demands we write "cough" when we're saying a word that sounds like "coff." Then, that same "ough" ending takes on a different sound altogether in a word such as "through." What if we simply *threw* our dictionaries *through* the window, and pleased the ghost of Mark Twain with our breezy, unfettered, original orthography?

This would be disastrous, for a simple reason: as difficult as English is to learn, communication would be harder if everyone spelled things every which way. SPOGG frowns on anything that makes language less clear. Having a uniform spelling for words makes a lot of sense.

Still, English has so many words. It's hard to count just how many, because some are variants of a single word, while others are no longer in use. But the *Oxford English Dictionary* lists 171,476 words that haven't fallen by the proverbial wayside (and there are many words beyond those that aren't included). Of these, as many as 25 percent are not phonetic, meaning they are not pronounced the way they're spelled. And even that is probably an overstatement of the help we get from the way words sound. A person from our nation's capital, for example, might say she cleans her clothes in a "warshing" machine, but when you ask her why she's putting an *r* in the word, she'll deny it. Bostonians have their own "idears" about how words are pronounced. We don't even know where to begin when it comes to the South, though we admire how many syllables they can give to a simple four-letter word such as "shit."

HOW WE GOT HERE: A BRIEF HISTORY OF THE ENGLISH LANGUAGE

One reason English spelling is so tough—a word that does not rhyme with cough—is that our mother tongue tangled with many fathers. If you were to sketch out a family tree, you'd first draw Germanic roots. Around the fifth century AD, Germanic tribes invaded the territory that is known today as England. Their language, Anglo-Saxon, is also known as Old English (and should not be confused with furniture polish of the same name).

Just before AD 600, the mother tongue took a Latin lover: the Christian monk Augustine, to be specific. Latin had been part of the language history of the region since Britain was sucked into the Roman Empire in the middle of the first century BC. But under the influence of Augustine, England converted to Christianity. This meant that Latin, the official language of the Lord (along with Greek and Hebrew), rose to new prominence. Latin had even more reason to seed the vocabulary after the Norman Conquest in 1066, which the pope blessed. More significantly, though, the invasion meant that Old English was Frenched, taking on many delicious Gallic words.

During the centuries after the Norman invasion, English was largely the language of the rabble. It didn't die out, but it wasn't being used to create great works of writing, either. The upper class and political leaders—including the king—communicated in Norman French, while scholars and religious leaders used Latin. It wasn't even until 1399 that Henry IV brought English back to the throne.

The three languages, though, weren't rigidly stratified. It was more as though they were braided together: one culture singing in three-part harmony. Businessmen were often trilingual. Given all this, it's no wonder French and Latin words have jumbled themselves with the original Anglo-Saxon ones, and why promiscuous English has so many interesting children.

Let's face it: English is a bit of a trollop, and spelling has never been her strong suit. Even our greatest writer, Shakespeare, spelled his own name a half dozen different ways. English appears to feel bad about her slatternly ways, though. She has an inferiority complex to Latin and Greek, and many spelling exceptions heed the Latin rules. Words that have a short stressed vowel but no double consonant "abominable," "habit," "hideous," "vomit"—are examples of English words with Latin envy.

Our alphabet adds to the challenge. It's Roman, which comes from the Etruscans by way of the Greeks. The oldest-known example comes from an inscription on a gold brooch dated to 600 BC. The Romans, in addition to being sentimental about their jewelry, were great conquerors, and managed to spread their letters and language across Western Europe. It's remarkable, really, that a writing system has lasted that long and been used for so many languages without a complete overhaul. A few letters have been added and dropped along the way, but it's fundamentally the same ancient alphabet, devised to represent a different set of words than the ones we write and speak.

Even the words that are still with us aren't necessarily pronounced the way they were when humans first coined them. Alphabets link symbols and the sounds they represent, but these links crumble over time as pronunciations change. We could easily do away with the letters c, q, and x and still be able to spell words like "kat," "kween," and "battle-aks," but that's a change easier discussed than brought about (and not only because of the way it would anger all those toddlers forced to learn the unnecessarily long alphabet song).

Also, spelling standardization is a relatively late notion. Before the printing press, words were handwritten, which sometimes led to copying errors. What's more, scribes were often paid by the letter or the line, giving them incentive to pad their prose. They also sometimes added letters to even out their line length. Also, many printers were Dutch. This is how the Dutch spell "mechanic": *werktuigkundige*. Need we say more?

During the three hundred years after the printing press

came into use, English experienced a massive vowel move-ment. This "Great Vowel Shift" of the fifteenth and sixteenth centuries transformed the way we pronounced our long stressed vowels (the ones called monophthongs, which can-not be broken down into smaller vocal parts). We literally started using a different area in our mouths to form these sounds.

While this was happening, people still continued to spell as they spoke. If you were to read a history of the language, such as the excellent *Inventing English*, by the Stanford Univer-sity professor Seth Lerer, you could see how the private correspondence of the age revealed a language in flux. French was losing its prestige, and English was emerging as the lan-guage of the land. In the midst of this, people who cared about language—scholars, pundits, public figures, and poets—debated whether English should be standardized. Spelling was among the topics: Should words be spelled as they're pro-nounced? Or in such a way that reflects their etymologies? It was quite a debate, taking into account history, culture, class, and aesthetics—considerations that preoccupy people who love language today.

Then in 1755, something both great and terrible happened to spelling: Samuel Johnson released his forty-thousand-word *Dictionary of the English Language*. His spellings weren't per-fectly consistent, and he tended to Anglo-Saxify words even if they had French origins. His goal wasn't to codify English, though. After spending enough time with it, he apparently concluded, as others had, that English, like the tides, was ruled by the moon. Even so, we still use many of his spellings, even as pronunciation continues to evolve.

CAN ANYTHING BE DONE ABOUT IT?

Over the years, many notables—Ben Franklin, Mark Twain, and George Bernard Shaw among them—have urged spelling simplification. Noah Webster, the American lexicographer, simplified many spellings in 1828 in his *American Dictionary of the English Language*. If you've ever wondered why Americans write "labor" while the Brits labour over a longer word, it's because of Webster's efforts. (He'd no doubt be appalled by American wedding invitations requesting the "honour" of your presence.) But even these simplifications weren't much considering the vast sprawl of our idiosyncratic spelling landscape.

Twain had many funny things to say about spelling reform, none of them optimistic. "It won't happen," he told the *Atlanta Constitution* in April 1906. "And I am sorry as a dog. For I do love revolutions and violence."

If publications did switch spelling on readers, he predicted, "the nation would be in a rage; it would break into a storm of scoffs, jeers, sarcasms, cursings, vituperations, and keep it up for months—but it would have to read the papers; it couldn't help itself. By and by, and gradually, the offensive phonetics would lose something of their strange and uncanny look; after another by and by they would lose all of it, and begin to look natural and pleasant; after a couple of years of this, the nation would think them handsome, sane, and expressive, and would prefer them to any other breed of spelling."

One newspaper, the *Chicago Tribune*, did tempt fate and the wrath of language purists, who argue that simplified, modern spellings divorce words from their etymological roots, depriving us of all sorts of history and nuance. We're sympathetic to this argument, though we believe that ease of use probably trumps nostalgia. Do any of those people still drive Model Ts or keep their milk chilled in an icebox? In early 1934, the *Tribune* rolled out twenty-four new spellings to its readership. A few stuck: "catalog," "analog," "tranquility," and "canceled." Many, though, look like kindergarten goofs. The word "jaz," for example, pleased the eyes of few fans.

THE *CHICAGO TRIBUNE*'S SPELLING SIMPLIFICATION LIST

During the next five years, the list expanded to seventy-nine, then shrank to forty. The *Tribune* stuck with this list, remarkably, until 1975. If you look at blurbs on the back of old books, the *Tribune* ones stand out with their use of "tho," "thru," and other simplifications:

advertisment	crystalize	lacrimal
altho	decalog	monolog
ameba	demagog	patroled
analog	dialog	pedagog
apolog	drouth	prolog
bagatel	eclog	skilful
burocracy	etiquet	subpena
burocratic	extoled	tho
canceled	fulfilment	thoro
catalog	genuinly	thru
controled	glamor	tonsilitis
controler	hummoc	tranquility
cotilion	instalment	
criscross	intern	

Ultimately, the effort was undone because teachers complained the simplified words were too hard for students to read. "Sanity may someday come to spelling," an editorial wrote, "but we do not want to make any more trouble between Johnny and his teacher."

For anyone not ready to give up on sane spelling, there is always the Simplified Spelling Society to join. Since 1908, this stalwart organization has advanced its case. So what if there's no end in sight to the war? With the rise of text-messaging and Internet shorthand, perhaps their day is about to arrive.

Meanwhile, the smart person will do the following: Study the list of commonly misspelled words; and learn some basic spelling rules and exceptions.

COMMONLY ~~MISPELLED~~ MISSPELLED WORDS

Plenty of words could be called commonly misspelled—"syzygy," for example. It's a delightful noun, which can mean the conjunction of three celestial objects; a pair of related things that are similar or opposite; or a poetic unit of two metrical feet (look, the metric system can get along with English measurements, after all). "Syzygy" regularly appears on spelling bee lists nationwide. But unless you're a poet, an astronomer, or obnoxious, you don't go around writing "syzygy" every day.

To make our list of commonly misspelled words, a word must also be regularly used by regular people, not by journalists, professors, or others who have reason to quote Gandhi (not Ghandi). Also, we have not included evil twins here. Those are words that sound alike, but are spelled differently. You'll find that list on pages 28–37.

Without further ado, the list:

acceptable

accidentally

accommodate (accommodations for four)

acquainted (don't forget the *c*)

acquire (ditto)

across (there is no *t* on the end)

all right (two words, except in rock lyrics)

a lot (two words)

amateur

angel (don't confuse this with angle)

apparent

argument

believe

business

calendar

canceled

candidate

careful

category

cemetery (eee!)

changeable (change doesn't change when it gets an ending)

collectible

committed/committee/commitment (a committee of four is just the right size)

conceivable

conscience

conscious

criticize

deceive

decision

definite/definitely (there is no ate in definite)

develop

different

discipline

dissatisfied

efficient

eligible

embarrassment (two *r*'s, two *s*'s)

equipment

espresso (there is no *x*!)

exceed

exhilarate

existence

extraordinary

feasible

fluorescent

forty

gauge

grammar (for the love of God, not grammer!)

grateful

harass

height

hierarchy

ignorance

incident/incidentally

independence/independent

interest

interrupt

irrelevant

irresistible

jewelry

judgment

labeling

lengthen

license

lightning

likable

manageable

maintenance (not maintainance)

medieval

memento

millennium

miniature

minuscule (not miniscule)

mischievous

misspell

necessary

nickel

niece

ninety

noticeable

occasionally

occur/occurred/occurrence

opportunity

parallel

pastime

permanent

pornography

possession

privilege

realize

receipt

recommend

repellent

restaurant

rhythm

ridiculous

safety

schedule

scissors

secretary

sensible

separate

shipment

significant/significance

specific/specifically

succeed

summary

surprise

suspicious

temporary

tendency

terrible

truly

twelfth

undoubtedly

useful
using
until
vegetable
villain (makes a good tattoo: see page 80)
warranty
weird
yield

SPELLING RULES, EXAMPLES, AND EXCEPTIONS

English spelling can be haphazard, but it isn't totally random, unless you're a kindergartner. Our own spelled the word "barfed" as "boft" until a classmate told her there was an *r* in the word. She then wrote "I borft" throughout an eight-page book describing her bout with a stomach ailment. In honor of this eight-page book, we offer you eight rules that, once learned, will help you spell thousands of words correctly.

To avoid the crimes, learn the rhymes:

The *I* Before *E* Rule
I *before* e
except after c
or when sounding like a
as in "neighbor" and "weigh."

More than a thousand words follow this rule. The exceptions also rhyme:

Except "seize" and "seizure,"
and also "leisure,"
"weird," "height," and "either,"
"forfeit" and "neither";
"financier"
doesn't rhyme here.
Damn.

Happier endings: seven more rhyming rules.

Very often, we can spell a root word with ease. It's when it marries itself to a new ending—a suffix—that we get into trouble. But suffixes need not cause us to suffer, if we can remember the rhymes that go with each rule.

Dear *E*, departed
When -ing comes to stay, little e runs away.
So a word like "freeze" becomes "freezing."

Another *E*-scape
If the ending starts with a vowel or a y,
the silent e then goes bye-bye.
Example: rake + ing = raking.

The Cowardly Lion Rule
In just two cases, the e does stay:
When the suffix starts with an o or an a
and the original word ends with ge or ce,
so courage + ous yields courageous.

Some Words Get a Double Consonant When You Add an Ending. Wonder Which to Double? Learn the Rhyme to Save Some Trouble.

If a word has just one beat
then the solution's really neat:
There, the consonant's simply doubled
and your spelling is not troubled.
When the syllable count is more than one,
this rule gets a bit more fun.
You listen where the word is stressed—
that's the secret to the test.
If the first one gets the weight
put just one consonant on the plate.
But if the second one is stressed
then doubling the consonant's usually best.

Examples: smother, smothered, smothering (the first syllable is stressed); omit, omitted, omitting (the second syllable is stressed); bat, batted, batting (a one-syllable root word gets a double consonant on its ending).

Some three thousand words follow these rules, so they're worth learning.

The Pursuit of Happiness

It's not Happyness, unless you're in Hollywood, home of happy endings and ungrammatical movie titles.

When a word does end with y,
you must trade it for an i

if the letter before the y
is not a, e, u, o, *or* i
except when the ending's -i-n-g.
In that case, let your letter y *be.*

Example: happy + ness = happiness; baby + ing = babying.
Some exceptions: day, daily; gay; gaily; lay, laid; say, said.

A Lesson Before Dying

Words that end in *-ie* change to *y* when they take the *-ing*
ending.

With -ie *words like die, tie, lie*
the -ie *turns into a* y
when blended with the -ing *ending.*
We promise you, we're not pretending.

Hitting the hard stuff

If you go picnicking, be sure to put the *k* before the *-ing*
ending. Words that end in *c* need that *k* to stay crisp in front of
endings that start with *e, i,* or *y*.

There's something called a special k
that inserts itself to save the day
with words that end in the letter c
but take endings that start with y, i, *or* e.
The k *keeps the consonant hard*
when you're picnicking in your backyard.

Example: frolic + ing = frolicking.

A LIST OF SUFFIXES

Suffixes are endings. The word "suffix" comes from a Latin term that means to fasten underneath. But rather than think of a suffix as some sort of verbal brassiere, we look at the lot of them as condiments. When added to root words, they extend and enhance the meaning of the original word. Just as mustard has no business being splashed on an apple, not all suffixes can be attached to all words. Alas, this prevents such words as "barffully" from entering the proper English realm, but even so, there is much that can be created with a proper suffix. We've listed some common word endings and provided examples of how they work below:

-able	drink + able = drinkable
-age	rough + age = roughage
-al	element + al = elemental
-ance	dally + ance = dalliance;
	deliver + ance = deliverance
-ary	vision + ary = visionary
-ate	blow + ate = bloviate
-cian	electric + cian = electrician
-ed	barf + ed = barfed
-ence	converge + ence = convergence
-er	sick + er = sicker
-est	deep + est = deepest
-ful	care + ful = careful
-fully	hope + fully = hopefully
-hood	child + hood = childhood
-ible	eat + ible = edible

-ile	infant + ile = infantile
-ing	say + ing = saying
-ish	tickle + ish = ticklish
-ly	love + ly = lovely
-ment	excite + ment = excitement
-ness	happy + ness = happiness
-ous	cavern + ous = cavernous
-sion	divide + sion = division
-th	strong + th = strength
-tion	educate + tion = education
-y	ease + y = easy

PLURAL TROUBLE: BREED 'EM AND DON'T WEEP

It should be so easy to turn a word into words. Usually, it is. For most, you can just add *s*. The exceptions:

Nouns That End in *ch*, *s*, *sh*, *ss*, *x*, and *z*. These nouns must add -*es* before they are to multiply. "Witch" becomes "witches." "Bus" becomes "buses." ("Busses" mean kisses, and we like to keep these things separate, even if some dictionaries let you go both ways.) An odd little word like "fez" becomes "fezzes." (It needs that double consonant in order to obey the double consonant rule on page 74.)

The Fairy tale rule: His *wife* cut a *loaf* of bread in *half* with a *knife*, and put it on a *shelf*. Then, a Maple *leaf*–covered *thief* stole a *calf*, while an *elf* ran for its *life* from a *wolf*. All the italicized words get a -*ves* plural ending. So wives, loaves, halves, knives, shelves, Maple leaves, thieves, calves, elves, and lives.

The Dan Quayle Rule: If it ends in *o* in the singular, then it gets an -*es* in the plural. "You spell potato, I eat potatoes."

The "Sometimes *Y*" Rule: Remember that *y* is sometimes a vowel? When it is acting like one, and is pronounced as its own syllable, it turns into an *-ies* ending in the plural. So "baby" becomes "babies," and "cry" becomes "cries." And boy, do they.

A WORD ABOUT STYLE

When is a spelling error not an error? When it's a matter of *style.* In some ways, the thing that editors refer to as "style" is like junior high school. Back then, you *thought* the pants you were wearing were just fine: normal blue jeans that were neither too long, too short, too baggy, nor too snug. You had no clue that anything else even mattered. But then, painfully, you found out your pants were not Levi's, specifically, those of the 501 variety. Was it written down somewhere that any jeans other than these were for idiots? We don't know; we never did manage to find any fashion rule book.

Publications, however, make their style books a bit more accessible, probably because most of the people who worked there were the sort to wear the wrong kind of jeans in junior high school, while their sneering peers went on to jobs in sales. If you work at a newspaper following AP style, for example, you know to spell "adviser" with an *-er* ending, not that amateurish *-or* that so many people try to append to the word. No doubt the high-pressured salesmen—excuse us, sales advis*ors*—still wear those 501 jeans.

Criminally Bad Spellers

*

Scarlett Johansson is no stranger to the phenomenon of extra letters. Her cup runneth over here (and elsewhere—but this is not that kind of book). So it is perhaps no surprise that she once covered her face with a piece of cardboard on which she'd written, "I'm being harrassed [sic] by the person taking this picture." It was clever of her to avoid writing "paparazzo," and instead call the photographer "the person taking this picture." Alas, she should have gone with "bothered" instead of a tough word such as "harassed," which has only one r.

Still, she didn't get anywhere near the teasing her peer Lindsay Lohan did when she signed off her Robert Altman mourning letter, "BE ADEQUITE." Her completely inadequate spelling gave us a rare opportunity to use the word "ironic." And then she went off to rehab, repeatedly.

It's not as though celebrities invented misspelling, though. The twentieth-century spelling doyenne Edna L. Furness, an English professor at the University of Wyoming, noted that a telegraph company that misspelled a name was sued for $5,050 in damages because the misspelling delayed delivery. Adjusted for inflation from the time that people still used telegraphs, we believe this is equivalent to roughly $1 zillion today.

Homicidal maniacs have also staked their claim in Cantspellvania. Convicted murderer Charles Manson, a fan of Japanese full-body tattoos, sent a letter from his jail cell to a guy who'd founded a tattoo museum in Japan. In it, Manson wrote the following completely incomprehensible message (we've put errors in boldface, but we still have no idea what he's talking about):

> Looking **DEEP, LONG**, now **becomeing** wonder in the mind **Now** is when as its always been **writen** in the **SUN**. Right **ON**. I been **comeing HOLY WAR** as **Gods Marks** say behold words. **Nows** the 1940s Hall of prisons in the USA. When behind the **judges** chambers the English words came that Japan was **to be hung** for crimes. Then **Crime** became the war behind the **merrows** of minds in forever.

Speaking of tattoos, several news outfits in 1999 reported the sad story of a twenty-three-year-old Michigan man who'd wanted "villain" to be inked on his arm forever and ever. The tattoo artist, not sure how to spell the word, asked his coworkers and the client. Rather than hunt down a dictionary, the lot of them decided "villian" looked right. It wasn't. The young "villian" ended up spending $1,900 on plastic surgery, and later sued for $25,000.

Some real-life villains can even blame their captures on their bad spelling. A San Francisco would-be robber went to a Bank of America branch and filled out a deposit slip with the following message: "This iz a stickup. Put all your muny in this bag." He worried that someone had seen him write the note, though, so he went to the Wells Fargo across the street and handed it to the teller there. She figured correctly that anyone who'd write a note like that must be an idiot. She then told him she couldn't cater to his demand because it had been written on a Bank of America form. He left, and got back in line at Bank of America, where police—summoned by the Wells Fargo teller—handcuffed him.

Meanwhile, a young New Jersey woman was convicted recently of drugging, shooting, and dismembering her thirty-nine-year-old husband, then dumping his body (inside a trio of matching suitcases) into the Chesapeake Bay. Why did police suspect her? They compared notes she'd written to her friends with anonymous letters they received about the murder. Her notes and the killer's letters had the same linguistic fingerprints. To wit: Both the killer and the suspect abbreviated "with" as "w/," and used a plus sign instead of the word "and." Both also misused dashes and quotation marks, and went overboard with commas. The woman now faces thirty years to life in prison. So let the record reflect that bad grammar and spelling can, indeed, be a matter of life, if not death.

THE DEVIL'S IN THE DETAILS: SPELLING ERRORS WE TAKE FOR GRANITE

Late in 2006, a six-ton granite monument to the Ten Commandments appeared mysteriously at the courthouse in Dixie County, Florida, as if deposited there by a mighty divine being. Unfortunately, he misspelled "adultery" as "adultry." And, unless he was fresh off a writing seminar with James "A Million Little Pieces (of Sentences)" Frey, he also badly botched the syntax of Commandment No. 4, writing, "Remember the Sabbath day. To keep it holy." It's as we've said all along: God is better at biology and geography than he is at spelling.

SEEN IN THE CLASSIFIEDS

REMODELED New Kitchen, Bathroom, Carpet and Tile. Great Location by the Falls. Many amenities; 2 pools, multiple tennis courts, 2 clubhouses. Rent to **Owen** option available. Call 305-555-6584.

Rent to Owen? To Owen Wilson? We'd love to live next door.

Grammar: It Ain't What It Used to Be

From an advertisement for apartments to rent: "Historic Pascoag **Grammer** School Apartments, Owned and Constructed by Excel Management." Do you think they'd rent to Owen? That really would excel.

PARTING THOUGHT FROM LORD CHESTERFIELD TO HIS SON, IN A LETTER WRITTEN NOVEMBER 19, 1750

You spell induce, enduce; and grandeur, you spell grandure; two faults of which few of my housemaids would have been guilty. I must tell you that orthography, in the true sense of the word, is so absolutely necessary for a man of letters, or a gentleman, that one false spelling may fix ridicule upon him for the rest of his life; and I know a man of quality, who never recovered the ridicule of having spelled wholesome without the w.

Errare humanum est...
to forgive is swine.

4.

Vulgar Latin and
Latin Lovers

*1992 is not a year I shall look back on with undiluted pleasure.
In the words of one of my more sympathetic correspondents,
it has turned out to be an "annus horribilis."**

—*QUEEN ELIZABETH II*

Away with him, away with him! He speaks Latin.

—*SHAKESPEARE, 2 HENRY VI, 4.7*

**The Society for the Promotion
of Good Grammar**

Dear Founding Fathers:

We're happy with the work you did on our Constitution, with one exception: there's so darned much Latin
in it that we're afraid some people have no idea what

---

* Note: it's "annus" not "anus." Filthy.

you're talking about, and as a result, might violate some of the Constitution's principles without even knowing it.

Specifically, we are troubled by your use of the expression "Writ of Habeas Corpus."

You say this shall not be suspended, except during rebellions or invasions. Your average American will look at that and say, "Who's Habeas Corpus, and why should I care about his writ . . . whatever that is?"

We humbly suggest, if you should ever rise from the dead to revise your noble document, that you simply write, "People accused of crimes are allowed to appear in court to make sure there's a legitimate legal reason to imprison them."

This will make sure the United States never sets up prisons where people are held indefinitely without having access to lawyers, and without being formally accused of specific crimes.

Not that such a thing would ever happen, of course, especially not here, where we all agree that all men are created equal, with a right to life, liberty, and the pursuit of happiness.

Sincerely yours,

SPOGG

P.S. Don't be surprised, upon your resurrection, to discover that we no longer write "chuse." It's "choose," with two *o*'s. But we think your way is perfectly charming.

What's not to love about Latin? It comes in so many flavors. There's ancient Latin, both proper and vulgar. There's Medieval Latin, and Modern, too, though the latter sounds positively oxymoronic, if we may be permitted to insert a Greek word thus. There's pig Latin, which isn't really Latin at all; nor is it pig, as long as we're in the mode of full disclosure. Even so, Benjamin Franklin still saw fit to write using it on occasion.

But let us now turn to serious matters,* specifically, the serious matter of Vulgar Latin. Once, Vulgar Latin was what John Q. Publicus used to chat with his neighbors in the waning days of the Roman Empire. It was not the sort of formal language carved into stone as a permanent monument to an idea or person.

We have our own meaning in mind for the term. Well, three, if you count the Latin translation of the children's picture book *Walter the Farting Dog (Walter Canis Inflatus)*. That's vulgar, indeed![†] But even that is not nearly as bad as Latin that is misused, e.g., when people say "i.e." when they mean "e.g." or "excetera" when they mean "et cetera." To use a Latin word, this nauseates us. And finally, the third sense of Vulgar Latin: language designed to impress, rather than to inform.

But let us back up a moment. In the last chapter, we learned that Latin meshed with Anglo-Saxon during the time of the Roman Empire, and again when the Church planted its roots in British soil. This made Latin the language of both the lordly and the learned. The same holds true today, in more ways than

---

* Are you sad we didn't put Horace's famous quotation in Latin? Weep no more. Here it is: *Amoto quaeramus seria ludo.*

† And an anus horribilis, to boot.

one. On the Scholastic Aptitude Test, for example, students who know Latin earn better verbal scores than students who don't. It's also easy to see the rampant presence of Latin in our biological classification system. Scientists have used the language this way since the Middle Ages, when scholars translated common animal names into long and complicated Latin ones. In the mid-1700s, the Swedish naturalist Carolus Linnaeus refined the system further into something called "binomial nomenclature," in which the first word is the animal's genus, and the second describes a certain notable characteristic, the animal's location, or the person who discovered it. Latin works nicely for these purposes because it is both precise and straightforward. The words mean what they say they mean, though naming the puffball mushroom *lycoperdon* (wolf fart) is probably more vivid than necessary, and we hope never to meet a *Vampyroteuthis infernalis* (vampire squid from hell).

Still, you might have stumbled over some of the more ponderous words in the previous paragraph. Genus? Binomial nomenclature? Is it even possible to say stuff like this without sounding a bit sniffy? Why not just say "group" and "two-word naming system"? To the Anglo-Saxon ear, this ancient polysyllabic spree comes across as pompous, designed to intimidate with erudition, so to speak. It is the difference between asking and inquiring or thinking and contemplating, or the difference between a dog and a canine or an ass and a posterior. Perhaps this aversion to these more formal sounds is some ancient instinct plowed deep in our marrow. Remember, Anglo-Saxon was for centuries at the bottom of the language heap in England. Who likes an overlord?

Unless you want to sound like one, choose your words carefully. If you write and speak using blunter, shorter Anglo-Saxon words, you can count on sounding straightforward (though in some cases, crude). There are exceptions if you're writing for scientists or lawyers and need the precision that Latin affords. But if your aim is simply to impress, we roll our eyes at you. We give you grudging permission to go ahead and use both Latin expressions and Latinate words. But we issue the following *caveat*: Reaching into your fancy-word bag and pulling out the wrong one will make you look like a poseur, if not a posterior.

FOR LATIN LOVERS: HELP WITH COMMON LATIN PHRASES

a priori (AW-pree-OR-ee)—"from the former." Thanks to the efforts of Immanuel Kant, this expression has a specific meaning in philosophical circles: something you needn't experience to know. You might have a priori knowledge, for example, that a romantic comedy starring Steven Seagal and Paris Hilton as star-crossed astronauts is going to stink, even if it's still worth seeing for the unintentional comedy. In mathematics and logic, *a priori* means something known or guessed before you work through the solution. The opposite of this—a posteriori—might sound like a fancy way to say "a rear end," but this is not the case. Rather, it's an answer determined after you've gone through each step of the solution.

ad hoc (add-hock)—for this purpose. An ad hoc committee is a temporary one.

ad hominem (ad-HAW-min-um)—"to the person" or "against the man." It's often used with "attack" to mean a personal attack. But it has a deeper connotation: to discuss the personal at the expense of the philosophical. We see this all the time in politics, as when Arnold Schwarzenegger called members of the California legislature "girlie men." (Note: SPOGG believes this expression should be spelled "girly men" because that means girlish, while "girlie" with the -*ie* ending connotes nudity. The California legislature is many things; naked is not one of them, at least not while on the job.)

ad infinitum (ad-infin-EYE-tum)—endlessly.

ad lib (add-LIB)—off the cuff, a shortening of *ad libitum* (which means "at your pleasure"). The verb form, to ad-lib, requires a hyphen.

ad nauseam (add-NAW-ze-um)—to a sickening extent. If you combine "ad infinitum" and "ad nauseam," you could wind up with infinite vomit. And if you add "ad lib" for "off the cuff," well, you'd probably need a new shirt.

addendum (uh-DEN-dum)—an addition to a statement, usually made in writing; literally "something that must be added." The correct plural for this is "addenda."

alma mater (all-muh-MOTT-ur)—"nourishing mother." Your college is your alma mater. We hope she nourished you with more than beer, although a single can does provide 4 percent of your daily carbohydrate requirement.

alter ego (ALL-tur EE-go)—alternative personality (literally, "another I"). Not "altar ego." That's what you call a misbehaving bride.

animus (ANN-im-us)—motivation or hostility. Animosity, of the sort one feels toward a restaurant after getting food poisoning that leads to *nauseam ad infinitum*, comes from this word.

bona fide (BONE-a-fide)—with good faith, or authentic;

genuine. Does this remind you of a dog treat? It's no coincidence so many dogs have been named Fido. In Latin, the word means "I obey," and the adjective *fidus* means "faithful." Almost implausibly, "fido" has two more meanings, separate from Latin, but so good they cannot be ignored. The first is a coin with a minting error, where FIDO is an acronym for "freaks, irregulars, defects, and oddities." The second acronym, used during World War II, stood for "Fog Investigation Dispersal Operation," where gasoline was poured into troughs alongside fog-shrouded runways. The flames would raise the air temperature and burn away the fog.

carpe diem (car-pay-DEE-um)—seize the day. After the movie *Dead Poets Society* came out in 1989, millions stood on desktops and urged extraordinary living. In response, Goths started publishing the magazine *Carpe Noctem*, which means seize the night.

caveat emptor (CAV-ee-at-EMP-tor)—"let the buyer beware." (Note: The first syllable rhymes with have. It's not pronounced KAWV-ee-ott, though enforcing this is more a matter for the People for Proper Pronunciation, should such a society be established.) In an age of Craigslist, eBay, and online Viagra sales, this is an especially important bit of Latin to know.

cogito, ergo sum (KOH-gih-toe-AIR-go-SOOM)—"I think, therefore I am." This notion is a pillar of Western philosophy, written by the French philosopher René Descartes. Later, the red-nosed comedian W. C. Fields paraphrased this as, "I drink, therefore I am."

curriculum vitae (cur-ICK-you-lum-VI-tee *or* cur-ICK-you-lum VEE-tie)—the "course of life." This is a glorified résumé. Where a résumé is a one- to two-page summary of your work experience and education, your "C.V." is longer and contains more information: your education, teaching and research experience, publications, awards and honors, and any groups you belong to. Use your curriculum vitae if you're seeking an academic job, fellowship, or grant, or if you're looking for work overseas. Or, use it if you're a pompous twit. Many international employers will expect that sort of thing (a C.V., not that you will be a pompous twit).

de facto (dee-FAC-toe or day-FAC-toe)—in fact, in reality, literally "from what is done" (whether it's legal or not).

epluribus unum (EE-PLUR-i-bus-OO-num)—out of many, one. Former vice president Al Gore got this one backward in a speech, saying it means "out of one, many." There are now twenty-seven thousand pages on the Internet that enshrine this error—a high price to pay for vulgar Latin.

e.g., which stands for *exempli gratia*—for example. You can remember this by pretending that e.g. stands for example given. *I like big dogs, e.g., Golden Retrievers and Germam, Shepherds.* Enclose it in commas when you use it.

ergo (UR-go)—so, therefore. You say "ergo," ergo you're a pompous twit. Put that on your C.V., why don't you.

erratum (eh-RAH-tum)—an error. The plural form is "errata." It's bad enough when people correct your errors; it's infinitely worse when they call them errata. Unless you aspire to pomposity, avoid this word.

et cetera/etcetera (ett-SET-ur-a)—and so on; literally, "and the rest." Note: There is no *x* in et cetera. Ergo, there is no reason for anyone to say "excetera." The abbreviation is etc., not ect.

ex cathedra (ex-kuh-THEE-druh)—with authority, or officially uttered (literally, "from the chair"—of the pope, no less).

ex libris (ex-LEE-bris)—from the library of (literally, "from the books of"). Note: this has nothing to do with the zodiac sign Libra, though that's also a Latin word, meaning balance or scales.

ex post facto (ex-post-FACT-oh)—applied retroactively (literally, "from what is done afterward"). For the love of Jupiter, do not say "expo-facto," as if you're talking about some sort of home show in a stadium. Lawyers are most likely to be concerned with this term, because an ex post facto law makes something that was previously legal illegal, and a person could be prosecuted (though unfairly) for having broken a law that wasn't yet a law. There is also an episode of *Star Trek: Voyager* that deals with "ex post facto." This alone should make you leery of using it in everyday conversation.

fiat (FEE-ut)—official sanction or arbitrary order (literally, "let it be done"). Also, as an acronym for Fabbrica Italiana Automobili Torino, the name of an Italian automaker that manufactures the Fiat Panda, a car that eats shoots and leaves. (Just kidding! It runs much better on gas.)

habeas corpus (HAY-bee-us-KOR-pus)—an order permitting a detained person to appear in court, usually to see if the detention is lawful. The literal translation is "you may have the body" (and we hope it is still a live one).

i.e., which stands for *id est*. (ID EST)—that is. Use this when you're explaining something. You can remember this by pretending that the i.e. really stands for "in essence." *I like cats and dogs, i.e., animals you can teach to go to the bathroom outside.* Enclose it in commas when you use it.

in loco parentis (in-LOH-koh-puh-REN-tis)—in the place of a parent. It does not mean "my mother is loco/insane" even though that is likely to be true.

in toto (in-TOE-toe)—entirely, as a whole. When the Wicked Witch of the West said, "And your little dog, too," to Dorothy, she could have said, "And Toto in toto," and meant the same thing.

ipso facto (IP-so-FAC-to)—because of that very fact. The band Badly Drawn Boy says "ipso facto" in its song "Something to Talk About." Ipso facto, we are talking about it here.

literati (lit-tur-OTT-ee)—lettered people, as in well read, not in possession of high school letterman's jackets.

magnum opus (MAG-num-OH-puss)—great work. In *Charlotte's Web*, Charlotte A. Cavatica (Latin for "of caves") called her egg sac "my magnum opus, my great work, the finest thing I have ever made." Not too shabby, for a spider.

mea culpa (may-uh-KUL-puh)—Latin for "my bad." People have been apologizing this way for nearly eight hundred years.

modus operandi (MOH-dus-aw-pur-AND-ee)—a way of doing something (or mode of operation). Cops are fluent in this Latin expression.

ne plus ultra (NEE-plus-UL-truh)—the pinnacle of excellence; literally, "beyond which there is nothing." It also sounds like a brand of stain-removing laundry detergent.

nolo contendere (NO-low-con-TEN-du-ree)—"I do not wish to contend." In court, this means you're not saying you did it, but you will accept your just deserts* (you guilty bastard).

non sequitur (non-SEK-wit-ur)—"it does not follow"; an incongruous statement. The pineapple is a symbol of hospitality. (Oh, sorry for that non sequitur. But it's true. And people

---

* Note: Not "just desserts." This is about punishment—getting what you deserve—not baked goods.

used to think tomatoes were poisonous. Many children still do!) Also, this is an obsolete meaning, but "non sequitur" at one point meant part of a collar—a part that no doubt would come clean when washed in ne plus ultra.

per capita (purr-CAP-it-uh)—for each person (literally "for heads," but not "forehead"). *Caput* means head. This is not to be confused with *kaput*, which means broken. If one is decapitated, though, one's caput is kaput. Capisce? (See "veto," page 97.)

per diem (purr-DEE-em)—by the day, every day. This is a good term to know when one is traveling on the company dime. It's the amount of food, drink, and lodging you can put on your expense report.

persona non grata (purr-SOH-nuh-non-GROTT-uh)—an unwelcome or unacceptable person. There are so many better ways to say this sort of thing. (Beslubbering dog-hearted flea, anyone?)

per se (purr-SAY or pear-SAY)—by itself, intrinsically. It is also a restaurant in New York City, run by a chef who worked at Napa Valley's famed French Laundry. (Do you think this restaurant, the pinnacle of excellence, washes its linens in ne plus ultra?)

postmortem (pohst-MOR-tum)—after death. In which case, may you *requiescat in pace*.

postpartum (pohst PAR-tum)—"after birth." This two-word phrase is not the same as afterbirth, the common word for the bloody birth organ called the placenta, which comes from the Latin word for cake.

postscriptum (pohst-SCRIP-tum)—postscript. P.S. You probably knew that already.

prima facie (PRY-muh-FACE-ee)—at first glance. A bit too cursory in connotation to be an alternative for "at first sight," the sort of love one feels for someone with a really prime face.

quidnunc (QUID-nunk)—a gossip or busybody (literally, "what now?"). Quidnunckery is the love of gossip. Perhaps because it was first written in 1709, when all the good gossip was about powdered wigs and bodice ripping, we urge its use today.

quid pro quo (quid-proh-KWO)—tit for tat. "Quid," meanwhile, is slang for a British pound (and a plug of tobacco). Quid pro tit (and presumably, tat) is illegal outside of Nevada.

rigor mortis (RIG-her-MORE-tis)—"stiffness of death." It's infinitely more colorful to say, "The stiffness of death has set in."

semper fidelis (SEM-pur fee-DAY-liss)—"always faithful." The motto for the United States Marine Corps, the Swiss Grenadier Regiment, and the Plymouth Argyle Football Club, among others.

sic (sick)—"thus" or "so." Uppity types put it in brackets when taking care to reproduce errors faithfully in other people's grammar and spelling. It's a short way of saying, "Look at what this idiot wrote." The verb "sic," which means to attack, is unrelated linguistically, but we are not above using it for the sake of a pun, as in *Things That Make Us [Sic]*.

sine qua non (SIN-uh-kwa-NON or SIN-ay-kwa-NON)—indispensable (literally, "without which not"). Ironically, this expression is dispensable.

status quo (STAY-tus-KWO)—the way things are (literally, "the state in which").

tabula rasa (TAB-yew-luh-ROSS-uh)—blank slate (literally, "a scraped wax writing board"). Latin for "table" is *mensa*, which is the name of a club for smart, snobby people.

tempus fugit (TEM-pus-FEW-jit)—"time flies." Inevitably leads to the joke "Time flies like an arrow; fruit flies like a banana."

terra firma (tare-uh-FURM-uh)—solid ground (literally, "firm land"). While the Latin version of this phrase is pompous, the English translation is hopelessly clichéd. Why not just say land? Is "hollow ground" really enough of a concern that we need to qualify it with an adjective?

veni, vidi, vici (VEN-ee-VEE-dee-VEE-cee)—"I came; I saw; I conquered." In 47 BC, this was reportedly the sum total of Julius Caesar's State of the Empire Address. Demonstrating a bad case of verse vice (see "vice versa," page 98), the rapper Jay-Z refers to this classic quote: "I came, I saw, I conquered/From record sales to sold out [*sic*] concerts." Leave it to the modern Greeks—fraternity brothers—to jumble the phrase on their T-shirts. Ergo, beware Greeks bearing the following message: *vidi, vici, veni*.

verbatim (vur-BAY-tim)—word for word; pronounced. *Verbatim* magazine, a language quarterly, is a favorite of SPOGG. See VerbatimMag.com.

veto (VEE-toe)—"I forbid." With 635 total vetoes, Franklin Delano Roosevelt was the most forbidding of U.S. presidents. This word should not be confused with the name Vito, which reeks forbiddingly of Mafia, concealed weapons, and death kisses. In Latin, though, *vito* means life-giving.

via (VY-uh)—by way of. The first syllable rhymes with "pie," not "pee." Go ahead and use this word; just pronounce it correctly.

vice versa (VICE-uh-VURS-uh)—the other way around. Not to be confused with that other word "vice," which means an immoral habit. A verse vice, meanwhile, is a bad habit of rhyming, as exemplified by Fezzic in *The Princess Bride*.

For the Littlest Latin Lovers: Can You Match the Kid-Lit Classic with its Latin Translation?

Cattus Petasatus	Winnie the Pooh
Tres Ursi	The Cat in the Hat
Virent Ova! Viret Pirna	The Three Bears
Winnie Ille Pu	Alice in Wonderland
Alicia in Terra Mirabili	Peter Rabbit
Fabula de Petro Cuniculo	Green Eggs and Ham
Quomodo Invidiosulus	How the Grinch Stole
Nomine Grinchus	Christmas
Christi Natalem	
Abrogaverit	

LATIN IN JANE AUSTEN: PORTRAIT OF THE ARTIST AS A LINGUIST

It is a truth universally acknowledged that many grammar absolutes aren't really absolutes at all. This includes our admonishment to avoid Latin unless you want to sound hopelessly pompous. When pressed into service by a great writer such as Jane Austen, Latin can be used cleverly to develop both plot and characters.

A pair of Jane Austen-o-philes from the college of liberal

arts at Dakota State University have developed software called JALATIN, which they used to analyze the density of Latinate words in her work. In general, the more educated the characters were, the more they stuffed their prose with Latin, and vice versa. Austen's great dolts—Lydia and Kitty Bennet—used the fewest Latinate words of all (around 6 and 4 percent, respectively). Mary Bennet, also a dolt, but of the pretentious sort, flooded her speeches with about 34 percent Latinate words, narrowly beating out the unctuous Mr. Collins, who scored almost 30 percent.

Interestingly, the most sympathetic heroines, including Elizabeth Bennet, use the same Latin density as the narrator of *Pride and Prejudice*. But Lizzy's speech isn't uniform by any means. When she is upset, as when she learns that her sister has shacked up with Wickham, her Latin usage plummets from 25 to 9 percent. The romantic Mr. Darcy is a bit more pompous than Lizzy. In his letter to her he clocks just under 35 percent Latin, edging ahead of Mary. But as his heartstrings loosen, so does his prose. Toward the end of the book, he utters just 22 percent Latinate words, and we swoon. Thus, in the hands of an artist, Latin can be used to shade a character, color a scene, or simply set the reader's pulse to racing.

HOGWARTS SCHOOL OF WITCHCRAFT AND WIZARDRY . . . AND LATIN

Were the Romans closet magicians? Do Catholic priests know something the rest of us don't? If they were at Hogwarts, their

Latin knowledge would give them a huge advantage over us lesser mortals because a big chunk of Harry Potter's spells are based in Latin. Here are just a few examples:

Accio: I summon (as when, in *Harry Potter and the Goblet of Fire*, he summons his broom).

Amortentia: A love potion—*amor* means love.

Crucio: I torture. Bellatrix Lestrange uses this one on Harry Potter in the fifth book, *Harry Potter and the Order of the Phoenix*. Earlier, her Cruciatus Curse sent Neville Longbottom's parents to St. Mungo's.

Felix Felicis: *Felix* in Latin means lucky or happy.

Imperius curse: This curse subjects the victim to mind control by the perpetrating wizard. It comes from the Latin word *imperiosus*, which means domineering or dictatorial.

Lumos: In Latin, *lumen* means light.

Petrificus Totalus: Totally petrified. In *Harry Potter and the Half-Blood Prince*, this spell is used to turn people into stone (in other words, to petrify them totally).

Veritaserum: Truth potion, administered in *Harry Potter and the Goblet of Fire*. *Veritas* is Latin for true.

LATIN TENDER: IN THE UNITED STATES, LATIN IS THE LANGUAGE OF OUR LUCRE

Have you ever contemplated the mysterious words on the back of the U.S. dollar bill? They're Latin mottoes attributed to the great Roman playwright Virgil, who was thought to possess singular wisdom about forces that build and destroy nations.

If you have a dollar bill (from the Latin word *bulla*, for seal), flip it on its back. Note the text above the pyramid on the left: "ANNUIT COEPTIS." This means "God favored our undertakings." Below the pyramid, you'll see "NOVUS ORDO SECLORUM." This means "new order of ages," a concept President George H. W. Bush invoked in 1990 with his words "new world order," when he and Soviet leader Mikhail Gorbachev signed a historic treaty marking the end of the cold war.

On the right is the eagle, symbol not just of the United States, but also of the Roman state. The eagle holds an olive branch and arrows, classical symbols of war and peace, as well as a banner that says "E PLURIBUS UNUM": From many, one (right Mr. Gore?). It's worth noting, however, that Virgil's usage line "e pluribus unus" refers not to a federation of united people and their states, but to salad—in which the colors of garlic and green herbs blend together to make one. Delicious!

MEET THE INKHORNS

During the Renaissance, scholars looked to Latin and Greek when the English lexicon felt insufficient, giving us such words as "describe," "educate," "eradicate," and "encyclopedia." These words, summoned from wells by scribes, are called "inkhorns." This practice helped turn English into a monster language. Now that we have this fat book of words, though, it's worth remembering that longer words aren't necessarily better, and big ideas can often be best expressed with small words.

Here's a quick list of lengthy Latin words and their often shorter, often preferable Anglo-Saxon counterparts:

ANGLO-SAXON	LATIN
anger	rage
aware	cognizant
belly	abdomen
brotherly	fraternal
deadly	mortal/fatal
deep	profound
dog	canine
feeling	sentiment/sensation
forbid	prohibit/interdict
foxlike	vulpine
friendly	amicable
free	liberate
gift	present
guess	suppose/presume
help	assist
horse	equine
match	correspond
pig	pork
shy	timid
teach	educate
understand	comprehend
wish	desire
wrath	ire

abcdefghijklm
nopqrstuvwx
yz123456789
0!@#$%abcd
efghijklmnop
qrstuvwxyz12
34567890!@#
%^&*()?.".

THE GREATEST ROYAL LOVE STORY NEVER TOLD

5

$%&*#$ Punctuation

Her Majesty the Queen
Buckingham Palace
London, SW1A 1AA
UNITED KINGDOM

Your Majesty,

We are the Society for the Promotion of Good Grammar, an American organization that exists to advocate the proper use of English.

In the course of our life's work, we have come up with some questions we believe Her Majesty is best suited to answer.

1. American and British rules of punctuation differ. For example, in America, we put most punctuation marks inside the quotation marks. Your Majesty's people put them on the outside. We think the British way makes more sense. Is Your Majesty at all interested in

reminding Americans that we've borrowed our language from Her Majesty's grand nation, and that we should jolly well respect the original punctuation rules?

2. Does the same go for spelling? Did you feel just the slightest bit uncomfortable when you read "organization" instead of "organisation"? Or does Her Majesty secretly think "theater" looks better than "theatre"?

3. British grammar treats singular nouns that describe groups of people as plural; American grammar treats these as singular. Does this have anything to do with "the royal we"? Our curiosity begs your insight.

4. Did Her Majesty love grammar when she was a princess? We believe American students are eager to know.

Madam, I have the honour to remain
Your Majesty's humble and obedient servant,
Martha Brockenbrough
Founder, The Society for the Promotion of Good Grammar
http://spogg.org

Apparently the queen's job as a constitutional sovereign prevents her from giving opinions about British versus American grammar. It is as we suspected: Grammar is such a serious matter that an opinion expressed by the world's most beloved monarch could disrupt the long peace enjoyed by citizens of England and the United States. It could lead to murder, mayhem, and general madness—worse, even, than the sort that happens at soccer / football matches. Indeed, the future of the

BUCKINGHAM PALACE

14th July, 2006

Dear Miss Brockenbrough,

The Queen has asked me to thank you for your letter of 18th May, and I apologise for the delay in replying. Due to the high volume of mail received in recent weeks, correspondence has been dealt with in strict date order.

Her Majesty was interested to read that you have founded The Society for the Promotion of Good Grammar.

The Queen has taken careful note of your comments. I am afraid, however, that as a constitutional Sovereign, Her Majesty's position precludes her commenting on or giving her personal opinions on such matters.

I am sorry to send you a disappointing reply, but may I send my good wishes for the success of your Society.

Yours sincerely,

Mrs. Sonia Bonici
Senior Correspondence Officer

Miss Martha Brockenbrough.

civilized / civilised world might depend on it. We always knew grammar was of critical global importance. Now, we have proof. Thank you, your majesty. Long live the queen.

THE IMPORTANCE OF PUNCTUATION

When it comes to language, they say talk is cheap, and a picture is worth a thousand words. No wonder there are so many starving writers. Commas, on the other hand, can be ruinously expensive. A single misplaced curve cost NBC's fictional television lawyer Ed his job at a New York law firm, and sent him into the bowels of a bowling alley in Stuckeyville, Ohio. Apparently, this is justice for an error that cost $1.6 million, and the ultimate punishment to a New Yorker: having to live in the Midwest.

This sort of thing could never happen in real life, of course. That's because in real life, a misplaced comma is even more expensive. A Canadian utility company snagged by a rogue comma had to pay an extra $2.13 million in 2006 to lease its power poles. We're guessing the author was sent to Canada's equivalent of Ohio, the Yukon, where it's probably too cold even to bowl.

How bad was the misplaced comma? It's the sort of thing that would be easy to miss, like a stray poppy seed lodged between the bicuspids. The troublesome sentence said that the agreement "shall continue in force for a period of five years from the date it is made, and thereafter for successive five year terms, unless and until terminated by one year prior notice in writing by either party."

That comma after the five-year terms bit (which should have been hyphenated, but we digress) acted like a rhetorical church key, slicing open the sentence for loose interpretation. This unnecessary tadpole meant that the contract could be canceled *during* the first five years—the very opposite of what the utility company had in mind. That's the thing worth noting: when lawyers get involved, whether in Manhattan or Stuckeyville, it's not the intentions that count; it's how the writing can be interpreted. This is why it pays (or at least doesn't cost) to be punctilious about punctuation.

THE END OF THE LINE: PERIODS, QUESTION MARKS, AND EXCLAMATION POINTS

Writers didn't always need to fret about punctuation. The earliest writing had no punctuation, or even spaces between individual words. It was like never-ending kindergarten, with the capital letters and daisy-chained words, until the third century BC, when a librarian at Alexandria named Aristophanes of Byzantium invented early versions of the comma, the colon, and the period. Alas, his creations weren't universally adopted, proving that librarians have been the Rodney Dangerfields of the civilized world for millennia.

Even as late as the ninth century AD, spaces and punctuation weren't routinely inserted in prose. Inscriptions on Roman monuments sometimes used dots to separate words, and ancient Greek manuscripts sometimes separated blocks of text with horizontal lines called *paragraphos*, which explains where we got our word "paragraph."

What's more, early punctuation served a different purpose than our modern system of dots, curves, and dashes. Early on, writing was meant to be read out loud. Punctuation showed readers where to breathe. It still does that, but even more, it helps make our meaning clear. Look how punctuation can change the meaning of this familiar string of words:

A woman: without her, man is nothing.
A woman without her man is nothing.

Relatively speaking, it's a modern notion to use punctuation to clarify the syntax of a sentence—one we owe to Shakespeare's colleague Ben Jonson, who wrote a book called *The English Grammar*. Published in 1640, it is pimpled with errors and inconsistencies,* so perhaps it was good that Jonson had been dead for three years when it came out. In any case, we like to think it was his enthusiasm about punctuation that led him to insert a colon between his first and last names, calling himself Ben:Jonson, though it seems more likely he was copying the bishops and administrators at Oxford and Cambridge who did the same thing in their Latin signatures. Even better, though, is what he called the colon: the "double prick." Potty-mouthed punners couldn't ask for easier joke material. (It's remotely possible Ben:Jonson was making a dirty joke; "prick" has been slang for "penis" since at least 1555, though it wasn't until 1863 that the name Johnson was used colloquially for the same thing.)

Although writers finally had a modern way to use punctuation, they used a much heavier hand with the points and

---

* "A foolish consistency is the hobgoblin of little minds." —Ralph Waldo Emerson

swishes for nearly two centuries, inserting them at every possible opportunity until the English writer H. W. Fowler penned *The King's English*, where he wrote, "It is a sound principle that as few stops should be used as will do the work." Fowler detested too many punctuation marks (particularly periods and the short sentences they accompany, something he called "the spot-plague"). He also hated newspaper reporters' habit of "long sentences either rambling or involved," calling these "inexpressibly wearisome and exasperating."

Amen to that.

The very easiest marks to master are those we use to end sentences: periods, question marks, and exclamation points. Of course, that doesn't mean everyone gets this right, even in the most simple of places. We found ourselves in Baton Rouge, Louisiana, riding in an airport shuttle with a sign that said, "WELCOME [*sic*] ENJOY YOUR STAY [*sic*]." Because of this punctuation-parched sign, our enjoyment was slow in coming. Instead, we pondered the various marks that could have been put to use, and how a reader might interpret them:

WELCOME! ENJOY YOUR STAY! (Someone is happy to see us.)

WELCOME: ENJOY YOUR STAY. (All business.)

WELCOME . . . ENJOY YOUR STAY. (Has a bit of a come-hither feeling to it.)

WELCOME; ENJOY YOUR STAY! (Ah, the casual elegance of a semicolon, the enthusiasm of an exclamation point. It's like a feather boa with a kicky cocktail dress, a look not everyone can pull off.)

WELCOME—ENJOY YOUR STAY . . . (But between you and us, we wouldn't be surprised if you didn't.)

WELCOME. ENJOY YOUR STAY? (We hope. Oh, God. If we don't fill our rooms, we'll go out of business. Have a breakfast bar coupon.)

WLCM, NJOY UR STAY :-) (Sent from my BlackBerry wireless handheld.)

The Period

This is the singing fat lady of punctuation marks. When one appears at the end of a sentence, it's over.

With the period, there are only a few tricky things to remember:

One Period, Period. When there's an abbreviation at the end of a sentence, there's no need to double up on dots. *I Was a Zombie for the F.B.I.*, not *I Was a Zombie for the F.B.I..* (No matter how it's punctuated, though, this movie is a dog.)

Placement Test: Periods go inside any quotation marks at the end of a sentence. American English and British English disagree on this point, though Americans sometimes pull a Madonna and punctuate with an English accent. The Hollywood bigwig who wrote to Lindsay Lohan while she was working on *Georgia Rule* goofed repeatedly. He wrote:

I am now told you do not plan to come tomorrow because you are "not feeling well". You and your representatives have told us that your various late arrivals and absences from the set have been the result of illness; today we were told it was "heat exhaustion". We are well aware that your ongoing all night heavy partying [*sic*]*

---

* This should be "all-night heavy partying."

is the real reason for your so called* [*sic*] "exhaustion".

The Logic Round: Periods go outside of parenthetical expressions that come at the end of sentences. *He never returned my
book (the idiot).* But if the whole sentence is parenthetical, the
period goes inside it. (Like this.)

The period has other names, including dot and "full stop,"
which one does not often hear outside England or dinner parties held by college English majors. Dots come at the end of
abbreviated words, though not, apparently, for a certain actor
whose catchphrase showed an abundance of pity for fools. The
following would pose a punctuation challenge to anyone who
wasn't paying close attention in the eighties: The actor Mr. T
played Sgt. B. A. Barracus on *The A Team.*

The Question Mark

How old is the question mark? Not as old as questions
themselves. The *punctus interrogativus* has had its modern
shape and function since the 1600s, but first appeared in English in the eighth century as a squiggle over a dot. It was
rarely used then because the syntax of our sentences made it
clear when questions were at hand. Now, alas, we can't always
rely on that cue. One of our least favorite things is to come to
the end of a sentence that we thought was declarative, only to

---

* So-called needs a hyphen. *My So-Called Life* should never have been canceled, if
only because of the properly administered hyphen.

find it was an interrogative. It's like swerving to make the exit on the freeway: always an unnerving business, often accompanied by unattractive squealing. If only we could copy the Spanish, and start our interrogatives with upside-down question marks.

There are three tricks to the proper use of question marks:

1. Use it with direct questions only: *Who hacked Lindsay Lohan's sidekick?* An indirect question is too passive-aggressive to deserve an actual question mark. *I wonder who hacked Lindsay Lohan's sidekick.* Same goes for a demand masquerading as a question. *Would you kindly remove your Mercedes from my sidewalk.*

2. It's the writer's choice with rhetorical questions: *How did the Mercedes get on the sidewalk? Could the underage actress behind the wheel possibly have been drunk.* Was that a rhetorical question? If so, then it's up to you to determine whether it gets a question mark, a period, or an exclamation point. Craig Conley, author of *One-Letter Words* and the keeper of a surreal online sleep-journal written by a semicolon, urges the adoption of the rhetorical question mark, to make this easier for writers and readers. It looks like this:

$$⸮$$

Who could ever say no to that ⸮

3. Take care with quotation marks: The question mark, unlike the period, can rest either inside or outside the quotation marks. Here's how to decide:

Is the entire sentence a question? Then put it outside the

quotation marks. *Was it Robert De Niro who said, "you'll have time to rest when you're dead"?*

If the question is only part of the quoted material, but not applicable to the sentence as a whole, then keep it inside the quotation marks. *In* Meet the Parents, *De Niro said, "I have nipples, Greg; would you milk me?"*

A final note: A question mark doesn't necessarily signal the end of a sentence. If many questions come rapid-fire in a row, there is no need to capitalize the first letter of the word that follows midsentence question marks.

Are stiletto heels comfortable? sensible? sexy? We think they're more like torture.

Microsoft Word will make it challenging to do this, underscoring your phrases with a doubt-inducing green squiggle (the same goes for ending rhetorical sentences with a period). But this is where the art comes into the writing, isn't it . . . isn't it⸮

Exclamation Points

Like the question mark, the exclamation mark is a relatively modern bit of punctuation, pogo-sticking its way into text during the seventeenth century. It's also been called a "bang," a "screamer," and other names too filthy to print. Despite its riveting nicknames, not everyone is a fan. In *The Elements of Style*, Strunk and White offer the following starchy admonition: "Do not attempt to emphasize simple statements by using a mark of exclamation. . . . The exclamation mark is to be reserved for use after true exclamations or commands."

Apparently the founders of Yahoo! missed this lesson, with no apparent effect on their stock price. Equally sanguine are the residents of the English town Westward Ho! And what about the musical *Oklahoma!*? The film version won an Academy Award. (Though they did cut the song "It's a Scandal! It's a [*sic*] Outrage!" perhaps recognizing they'd crossed the bang barrier.)

It's safe to say the rest of us (and the creators of *Gutenberg! The Musical!* an actual musical about the inventor of the printing press) can't count on riches, tourist activity, or gold statuettes if we spear our prose with exclamation points, making shish kebabs of our sentences. It's best to use them to communicate surprise, anger, shame, protest, or some other high-volume emotion, and even then, just one at a time. Please!

TRULY POSSESSED: APOSTROPHES, SLASHES, AND HYPHENS

Though the exclamation point might have a case for unpaid overtime, the apostrophe is the only punctuation mark that's spawned its own protective society. (Defenders of the screamer take note: The UK-based Apostrophe Protection Society's home page includes eight exclamation points; it's possible this is seven too many.) The Apostrophe Protection Society has much work to do, however. The enemies of this useful curve of punctuation are many. George Bernard Shaw called them "uncouth bacilli." The English teacher Peter Brodie, who we can only assume had recently suffered a head injury, called them "largely decorative" in a 1995 issue of *English Journal.* Largely decorative? If his eternal reward is spent in Satan's hell, he'll come to appreciate the difference between decoration and damnation.

The R.E.M. guitarist Peter Buck, meanwhile, has said, "We all hate apostrophes." It might be unkind to point out that this is the same man who used the sleeping-pills-and-booze-made-me-crazy defense after dousing British Airways flight attendants with yogurt, but all's fair when punctuation is on the line. All the hating makes us miss the late Frank Zappa, who not only titled albums with apostrophes, but also titled one *Apostrophe(')* (which includes the wise song "Don't Eat the Yellow Snow" and the pleasingly hyphenated "Stink-Foot").

With all the animus, it's no wonder we've caught repeated apostrophe catastrophes in the wild:

The cover of *American Pastoral*, the Pulitzer Prize—winning novel by Philip Roth, contains the following text, attributed to powerhouse book critic Michiko Kakutani: "One of Roth's most powerful **novel's** ever . . ." (Kakutani got it right in the original *New York Times* review, so blame the editor of the book cover.)

The use of "DVD's" has appeared as the plural for digital video disc in the *New York Times*. The gray lady also used "subscriber's" when it meant "subscribers'" in a story about the difficulties customers of America Online have canceling their accounts.

Paris Hilton struts the streets in a T-shirt emblazoned with her trademarked, apostrophe-free catchphrase: "THATS HOT."

The captions on the TV show *Lost* at one point said, "you're husband" instead of "your husband." This usage would be correct only if used as a taunt in the spirit of "I'm rubber, you're glue . . ." So, "I'm husband, you're wife / stuck together, rest of life."

Meanwhile, an advertisement for Level vodka goes the other way and omits the apostrophe entirely, claiming to be the "**worlds** first perfectly balanced vodka," proving it's never wise to drink and punctuate.

Fortunately, it's not difficult to use apostrophes correctly. They have three functions: to show possession, and to indicate contractions and omitted letters.

1. Use an Apostrophe to Show Possession

This is the world's first perfectly balanced vodka. Cheers!

Most of the time, an apostrophe-*s* is all you need to form a singular possessive properly. Not everyone agrees with what to do for nouns ending in *s*, however. Do the bus' wheels go round and round? Or the bus's wheels? You will find people who make the case that *s'* is the proper ending, while others argue strenuously that *s's* is the only way to go, except with the case of certain ancient proper names, including Jesus, Moses, and O Mighty Isis. So what's a concerned user of the apostrophe to do? Besides writing around the problem (the wheels of the bus, the glossy hair of mighty Isis, the fuel-efficient car of Jesus), the best course is to pick one solution and stick with it. You might please only half of your readers, but the alternative is to dismay all of them. (SPOGG's preference here is to write the apostrophe-*s*, where the 's is pronounced as its own syllable.)

By the way, stodgy editors insist that inanimate objects can't have possessions. In most cases, this is unnecessarily restrictive. *Pirates of the Caribbean: At World's End* is a more resonant, more accurate movie title than *Pirates of the Caribbean: At the End of the World*. The sun's rays . . . the rays of the sun . . . use whatever suits your writing better. Very often, the shortest solution is the clearest. Do be careful, though, not to collapse your writing too much. *The hair of the dog that bit you* doesn't mean the same thing as *the dog's hair that bit you*. Regardless of how well balanced the drink, it's the mouth of the dog that bites, not the fur.

For plural possessives, add an apostrophe: First, form the correct plural. Bus becomes buses; chicken becomes chickens; Jones becomes Joneses. Then, add an apostrophe. So, it's the buses' drivers; the chickens' coop; and the Joneses' family reunion. The Hollywood movie *Two Weeks Notice* should have been *Two Weeks' Notice*.

Exception alert: Some plurals do not end in *s*; for those, you will need to add the apostrophe-*s*. "The women's sweaters" is an example.

No apostrophe with possessive pronouns: His, hers, its, theirs, yours, and ours do not get an apostrophe-*s*. They're already possessive. The most common error here is it's for its. Remember your towels, embroidered with his, hers, and its. No apostrophe is required. Indefinite pronouns (somebody's, anybody's, someone's) do get the apostrophe.

2. Use an Apostrophe with Contractions
Can + not = can't
Will + not = won't
Do + not = don't, etc.

3. Use an Apostrophe to Show Omitted Letters
1980s becomes '80s.

Gone fishin'.
The Beastie Boys "be illin'."

Do Not Use Apostrophes to Form Plurals, even with Initialisms

It's ABCs, DVDs, and IRAs. There is one possible exception, for plurals made from single letters. *I got all A's on my report card!* The Apostrophe Protection Society warns against this, but SPOGG thinks it's a reasonable way to differentiate A's from the word As.

Dear Albertsons [*sic*]

We sent this letter to Albertsons [*sic*] grocery store. Alas, no reply. We're beginning to think only Canadians and the queen have any manners.

The Society for the Promotion
of Good Grammar

Dear Albertson's grocery store:

We are the Society for the Promotion of Good Grammar, and we read with interest your online customer-satisfaction pledge, which says the following:

"If you are not completely satisfied, contact us and we will make it right for you. Guaranteed!"

We are writing to say that we are not completely satisfied with how you've spelled the name of your company. As your television jingle goes, "It's Joe Albertson's supermarket, but the produce department [bakery, oral hygiene aisle, what have you] is mine."

Perhaps you haven't noticed—this sort of thing can be like having your fly inadvertently unzipped—but you're missing an apostrophe in Albertson's. The name of your store is a possessive, not a plural (please refer to your jingle if you're in doubt). And even if it were a plural (perhaps if Joe's wife were in on the business), you'd still need an apostrophe, but on the other side of the *s:* Albertsons'.

In any case, we can't drive past your delightful store without feeling a little shiver of horror zoom down our spines. While an apostrophe isn't a product per se, we would like for you to make this right for us. Guaranteed! We're not asking for a refund, just an apostrophe, shaped like the stem of a delicious, crisp apple. From your produce department, naturally.

Sincerely,

SPOGG

The Arkansas Rule

In Bill Clinton's home state, recent legislation requires official state publications to print the possessive *Arkansas's* as so. It's not Arkansas'. Absolutely not. The eighty-one-year-old politician who drove the effort can now go gently into that good night knowing that the apostrophe and the silent *s* have been duly honored. All too often, that doesn't happen, and apostrophes get plugged into places where they have no business, like olives in blueberry pies (never pie's, despite how it appears on countless diner menus).

Address labels, Signs, and Party Invitations

Every day we pass a neighbor's house marked with an obviously hand-crafted sign. Someone went to a great deal of trouble burning FITZWANG'S into a large wooden shingle, only to ruin it with that altogether inappropriate apostrophe. It's not just the Fitzwangs who do this. Each holiday, we get letters signed with the equivalent of *Love, the Claus's*. And don't even get us started on return-address labels, printed incorrectly by the millions. Here are the correct variations:

We are going to the Fitzwangs' house.

We're visiting the Fitzwangs.

The Fitzwangs live here.

This is Debbie Fitzwang's home.

Love,

the Fitzwangs.

The Fitzwangs' correct mailing label:

The Fitzwangs

1313 Mockingbird Lane

Boopsylvania, PA

Slash/Burn

In an age of multitasking, the slash (aka the virgule) is a helpful bit of punctuation that traces its ancestry all the way to ancient Rome. Today, it's what enables someone to be a singer / songwriter, or a lesbian lover / DJ. The virgule also asserted itself in earnest with the Kirsten Dunst movie *Crazy /*

Beautiful.* One could not help but ask, "Which came first, you mysterious Hollywood auteurs, the beauty or the insanity?" When used like this, it shows words that have a close relationship with each other. You may also use it:

as a stand-in for "or";

as a line break in songs and poetry; and/or

to represent "per" (as in miles / gallon)

The Hyphen

English has used the hyphen since the late thirteenth century, though in medieval writing, it marked a word that had been split by the end of a line. Unlike today, those words weren't divided by syllable; scribes simply marked the break with a hyphen when they ran out of room.

If a slash is a mark of copulation, the hyphen is one of procreation. It is used to join words together as modifiers, a red-hot fusion that sometimes even results in the birth of a brand-new being. When the love-children of the joined pair are nouns, these start-up words can eventually even lose their hyphens altogether. Why, in some newfangled dictionaries, "startup" is a single word already. The television show *Extreme Makeover* is another example of two words that have been made over into something new.

What's more, hyphens aren't picky about the types of

---

* The felicitous use of the virgule only makes the incorrectly punctuated tagline more disappointing: "When it's real. When it's right. Don't let anything stand in your way." (Especially not periods hijacking the proper place of commas.)

words they'll hook up with. They'll do verbs (slam-dance); nouns (self-knowledge); verb-preposition combos (lean-to); and even compound adjectives. (I emerged from the lean-to with brand-new self-knowledge.) It's when linking modifiers that things get particularly festive: writers can form a veritable verbal daisy chain. It's a better-late-than-never proposition. Or, he's a peanut-butter-with-bacon-sandwich kind of guy.

Where hyphens abstain is when multiple-word modifiers come *after* their noun. So you would write "well-read man," but you would say "the man is well read."

Likewise, hyphens do not fraternize with adverbs. Adverbs modify adjectives, not nouns, and their relationship with the adjective is already made clear by that fact. So you would not write "hotly-contested issue"; it would be "hotly contested."

Just as it's important to avoid sticking your hyphens where they don't belong, it's also important to do a thorough job of inserting them where they are required. Otherwise, you might end up with the inadvertently creepy movie-poster problem. On signs advertising *The 40 Year Old Virgin*, an improperly punctuated movie title to begin with, marketers wrote *The 40 Year-Old Virgin*. It's as though the antihyphen/hyphen battle ended in a draw when they got to the poster part, and they decided to compromise with one instead of the two that good grammar requires. The result, unfortunately, makes no sense. What's more, it calls to mind an image of forty virgins, young enough to need diapers. No thanks!

PAUSE FOR CONCERN: COMMAS, DASHES, ELLIPSES, SEMICOLONS, AND COLONS

When we get to commas, dashes, ellipses, semicolons, and co-lons, punctuation has many powers. It helps us organize, sepa-rate, and gather our words to make their meaning clear. But it can do more. It can give groups of words rhythm, and through that, resonance. Here's how Chief Justice John Roberts, for ex-ample, used the dash to dazzle in one of his opinions: "The state did—nothing."

At least one ivory-tower fan went wild: "That little dash is brilliant," gushed Yale professor Akhil Amar. You can see his point. The jurist's prudent dash invites a pause just long enough to swing a spotlight of derision onto the poor state. The punctiliously placed pause turns words on a page into a human voice echoing in the reader's mind—not a mean feat for a quick stroke of ink. Of course, dashing toward brilliance is some-thing that can only be done with a solid grasp of how the vari-ous marks can be used. Without further ado:

Use a Comma

To string together short independent clauses: *We came, we saw, we conquered.* Note: If you have just two independent clauses, and particularly if they're longer than a few words each, you must use a semicolon or people will call this a "comma splice," a hideous expression that describes two complete sen-tences joined by commas. When the independent clauses are short, or when there are more than two of them stacked up, this practice becomes acceptable.

When addressing someone directly: *Mrs. Robinson, you're trying to seduce me.*

To separate items in a simple series: *The Lion, the Witch, and the Wardrobe.* Please note that many publications omit the comma before the "and." This is fine. You must be consistent about it, and also careful not to inadvertently change the meaning of your sentence. "Peter, Paul and Mary are here" does not mean the same thing as "Peter, Paul, and Mary are here."

Between two clauses linked by conjunctions (and, but, neither, yet, for, nor, and so): *It was the book my father used to read to me when I was sick, and I used to read it to your father.* (Note: with "and," you don't always have to use the comma. If the pause is helpful, go ahead and use it.)

As bookends on either side of appositives: These are phrases that act as explainers to the nouns they accompany. Paris Hilton's birthday-party invitation on MySpace neglected to insert the commas after Hilton and world, to stunningly bad effect (the unnecessary capitalizations are also hers):

Paris Hilton [sic] the Hottest Heiress in the world [sic] will celebrate her birthday on Saturday, February 17th.

Dash It all

Not all dashes are created equal. There's the en dash, which is the width of the capital N. And there's the em dash, which is just a tad wider. They differ more in function than in width.

Use an En Dash

To show number and date ranges, as well as distances

spanned: July–October; 6 p.m.–9 p.m.; Seattle–San Francisco; the score was 30–14.

To show stuttering: W–w–what's up, Doc?

The em dash, as Chief Justice Roberts showed us, is a bit more fun. This Craigslist ad missed a real em-dash opportunity:*

> *1980s most prominent soap stud's white couch set for sale. $10,000. White herringbone cloth on black legs with chair and ottoman. Cash or money order or certfied cashier's check only. Serious inquires only, duh!*

We wrote the actor the following letter.

The Society for the Promotion
of Good Grammar

Dear Soap Stud,

We enjoyed stud-filled soaps in the 1980s, so we are writing with more than casual interest in your couch, love seat, and ottoman. (Secretly, we're hoping you're Blackie. We never got the Luke thing.)

---

* If you're looking for used celebrity furniture or badly spelled ads, Craigslist is a treasure trove. We also found this. All spelling and capitalization errors are by the hapless assistant to the Famous Hollywood Producer [*sic*, *sic*, and *sic*]:

> Famous Hollywood Producer's Couch, Desk, and Office Furnature For Sale. All furnature must be gone by the end of the week. Set up an appointement to come by.

We sincerely wish you the best with your sale. We urge you, however, to correct your spelling and grammar. After all, you're asking for $10,000 for secondhand furniture, and in considering your line of work, buyers must beware the sort of use that couch might have received.

In any case, you're far more likely to get your money if you can demonstrate you know your way around a comma as well as fabric as improbable as "white herringbone."

It's "ottoman," not "ottomon."

"Cash, money order, or certified cashier's check" (note the *i* in certified) is more elegant than your "or, or, or" construction.

The interjection "duh" should be set off with an em dash. Or it should be its own sentence. The comma—duh—makes it a run-on sentence.

Very sincerely yours,

SPOGG

Use the Em Dash

To season your prose with pauses: It's less formal than a colon, less distracting than a pair of parentheses, and more dramatic than a comma. Observe:

- He uttered just one word: rosebud.
- He uttered just one word (rosebud).
- He uttered just one word, rosebud.
- He uttered just one word—rosebud.

To set off quotations: "Me fail English? That's unpossible."—Ralph Wiggum

To show an abrupt change—an unplanned pregnancy, perhaps, in a song lyric: Papa, don't preach—I'm in trouble deep. [And it's making me sing idiotic half rhymes.]

To set off a phrase that contains a series in it: He was a rogue—dashing, unreliable, and impetuous—and she liked it.

To indicate an unfinished thought, like this—

Note: Too many em dashes make your writing sound overly breathless. Also, some publications require a space around the em dash, while some do not. If you aren't under anyone's thumb, pick whichever style you like, and stick with it.

Read My Ellipsis

Britney Spears is a big, big fan of the ellipsis, y'all. In one of her "Letters of Truth," she used four:

> If anyone is a family person . . . it's me.
> Maybe this is the reason for this letter . . . to maybe allow people to look at me differently.
> I just want the same things in life that you want . . . and that is to be happy.
> I guess we will never really understand or figure out life completely. That's God's job. I can't wait to meet him . . . or her.

Of these, only the last is a good use. In our opinion, she should have used a comma for the first one, and dashes for the next two.

Outside Britney's world, an ellipsis has three uses:

To show an omission, as when a quote has been condensed. "I just want . . . to be happy."

To insert a really long pause.

To show a thought that's trailing off. "Why I ever married Kevin Federline is a mystery . . . ." (Note the fourth dot in that set. It's the punctuation at the end of the sentence.)

The Semicolon

Like pizza, the semicolon is a mouthwatering Italian import, used to make individual sentences stand a little closer to each other. How romantic! It entered English in the sixteenth century, through Shakespeare's sonnets and Ben Jonson's work, among other sources. Even so, many writers hate it. A columnist for the *Minneapolis Star Tribune* said this: "I think it's a worthless, clumsy, trashy mark with no redeeming stylistic value." The revered editor Michael Kinsley has banned semicolons outright. He told the *Financial Times* they should be replaced with periods, if only to keep people from spiraling into the uncontrollable addiction of bad usage. We quote:

> Drugs are banned sometimes because a minority of users will have negative side effects, or because taking them correctly is complicated. Actually, I'm opposed to that kind of thinking re drugs, but I am okay with it regarding punctuation. Punctuation can't save your life.

We're not so sure about that. While we haven't yet found direct evidence of punctuation being lifesaving, we have discovered that bad punctuation led to life in prison for a certain murderous New Jersey housewife who couldn't hold her semicolons (unlike the Son of Sam, who the journalist Jimmy Bres-lin called "the first murderer anybody ever knew who could use a semicolon"). The semicolon has played a role in the life sen-tence of marriage, too. When gay couples in San Francisco were temporarily allowed to marry, opponents of such unions tried to get the court to step in, only to lose out because of an ambigu-ous semicolon. Said the judge, "I am not trying to be petty here, but it is a big deal. . . . That semicolon is a big deal."

How big a deal? The monumental mark appeared in a sentence requesting the city of San Francisco to "cease and desist issuing marriage licenses to and/or solemnizing mar-riages of same-sex couples; to show cause before this court." As the judge read it, that semicolon stood in for an "or." He tossed out the petition, though the state later nullified the marriages anyway.

It wasn't even the first time a court case had swung on the curve of this particular mark of punctuation. The Texas Su-preme Court of 1870–73 was called "the Semicolon Court" af-ter it used a semicolon to nullify the contested election of a Democratic governor (who took office anyway).

Despite all the folderol, semicolons are simple to use. A semicolon can:

Join two closely related sentences: These are independent clauses that aren't already joined with "for," "and," "nor," "but," "or," "yet," or "so" (these are the coordinating conjunctions, which you can remember from the FANBOYS acronym). It's not just the official FANBOYS that the semicolon replaces; it stands in for all sorts of transitional expressions: "because," "in addi-tion," "at the same time," and "in fact," among others. *"I no longer study Kabbalah; my baby is my religion."—Britney Spears*

Separate items in a complex list (one that might already have commas in it, for example): *We love fantasy heroes, despite their physical flaws: Harry Potter, with his thunderbolt scar; Sunny Baudelaire, who has fangs and a limited vocabulary; and Frodo Baggins, who eventually loses a finger to Gollum.*

Note: unlike commas, semicolons go outside quotation marks.

Use a Colon

You already know about Ben:Jonson's double prick; here's how to use one correctly:

to introduce explanatory material or a list (see colon above);

to introduce a long quote;

to set off dialogue; or

between chapter and verse of the Bible, or hour and minute of time.

Note: colons go outside the quotation marks (unless they're part of the quoted material).

Should You Capitalize After a Colon?

Experts do not agree on this matter. There is no need to capitalize if the colon comes before an incomplete sentence. Some editors (particularly those who follow *The Associated Press Stylebook*) say you should capitalize if a complete sentence follows the colon. Others say this isn't necessary. Whatever you choose, just be consistent.

A LITTLE ON THE SIDE: PARENTHESES AND BRACKETS

We rather prefer the medieval parentheses to the modern version. Back then, the marks curved inward and the parenthetical material was underlined)<u>like this</u>(making it look like a secret tucked into an ample woman's bosom. Since the 1400s, though, parentheses have curved the other direction. Their use is simple—to set off extra material. The only real trick to them is punctuation, which goes outside the parenthesis (unless the entire sentence is an aside). (Like this one is.)

Brackets, meanwhile, should be used when adding information or interpretations to quoted material.

QUOTATION MARKS

Quotation marks are easy to use, and easier to abuse. They belong around directly quoted material. Though it's not ungrammatical, it's cheesy to use them to express irony, unless you're the sort who likes it when people talk with quote fingers.

Punctuation Rules with Quotation Marks:

In American English, periods and commas go inside the quotation marks.

Question marks and exclamation points go inside when they're part of the quoted material, but they stay outside when they apply to the sentence as a whole.

Set off direct quotes with commas UNLESS the quoted material is an incomplete sentence.

If your quote has more than one sentence, some publications recommend setting it off with a colon and line break, and dropping the quotation marks altogether.

For a quote within a quote, use a single quotation mark: *She said, "I love 'The Sound of Music,' but my favorite song is 'The Sounds of Silence.'"*

When you interrupt a quote with a speech tag, capitalize the second part of the quote only if it's a complete sentence: "I'll get you, my pretty," she said, "and your little dog, too." "I'm melting," she said. "I'm melting—what a world."

PUNCTUATION CITY, USA

More than twenty years ago, Hamilton, Ohio, decided to spice things up by adding an exclamation point to its name. Although the media paid attention, the people who counted—namely, the post office and the United States Board on Geographic Names—didn't. Now, the punctuation mark is mostly a memory for the plucky midwestern town.

If other cities care to follow in Hamilton's footsteps, we have a few ideas for which punctuation marks and typographic tricks they should use:

- Boston—(that's a long dash, in honor of the marathon)
- {Las Vegas} (with braces, because what happens in Vegas stays in Vegas)
- And what about Colonial. Williamsburg ("Colonial period Williamsburg")
- $an Franci$co (it's expensive)
- *Houston* (leans to the right)

- −cino, California (that's an en dash)
- DeKa#, Illinois (pound symbol, i.e., "lb")
- Minneapolis=St. Paul (twin cities of equal stature)

MALEDICTA!

When they see bursts of rapid-fire punctuation, readers of comic books know foul language is afoot. Called "maledicta," these naughty words made from asterisks, ampersands, exclamation points, and octothorpes are increasingly pressed into service in the columns of newspapers and magazines. When vice presidents drop the F-bomb, though, newspapers pussyfoot around the question of what to print. This is why SPOGG sent a solution to Norm Goldstein, editor of *The Associated Press Stylebook*. To our dismay, he did not reply, the B@$ + @®D.

The Society for the Promotion
of Good Grammar

Dear Mr. Goldstein:

The Society for the Promotion of Good Grammar has lately been pondering profanity. Despite our tremendous admiration for your work, we believe your recommended solution—replacing all but the initial letter with hyphens—creates problems undesirable to any news organization.

First, a hyphen's job is not to stand in for missing

letters. It links compound words and phrases, and tells readers when a word has been split at the end of a line. If hyphens had unionized, they would be right to object to standing in for filthy letters. It's not in their job contract.

More seriously, though, replacing letters with hyphens can make the epithet overly obscure, and thus introduce inaccuracies.

For example, if a politician said, "He is an ass-hat," and a reporter wanted to clean that up, your style dictates that reporter write, "He is an a------." Reasonable readers would interpret an *a* followed by six long-suffering hyphens to represent "asshole." The politician, however, never said "asshole." Instead of getting credit for adopting a fresh and comical epithet, he's cast into the gutter with the rest of the old-school potty mouths.

Similarly lost would be the difference between "fuckwit" and "fuckoff." We do not believe we need to convince a wordsmith such as you that these words are every bit as different as a feckless boss is from the relative who's parked himself on your couch for months on end. As you can see, the consequences for news organizations striving for accuracy are significant, especially living in a profanity-filled age such as ours.

We therefore propose a different system, which has the benefit of (1) looking snazzy; and (2) giving reporters reason to say "maledicta," which means words typed from punctuation and other common symbols. After all, if this solution is good enough for the funny pages, it should be good enough for the editorial ones.

And last but not least, this also is more equitable to the long-suffering, oft-abused hyphen.

MALEDICTA KEY

Vowels	Consonants
A = @	C = ©
E = {	D = 〉
I = !	F = #
O = Ω	H = ⋆
U = ¥	K = <
	L = £
	N = ^
	G = }
	P = ¶
	R = ®
	S = $
	T = +
	W = π

Together, these symbols allow intrepid journalists to type all seven of George Carlin's dirty words—along with several more modern compounds—in a way that avoids printing profanity, but leaves no doubt in the reader's mind what has actually been said.

If there are additional bits of profanity that our maledicta key does not cover, do not hesitate to contact us. We would be happy to expand on our work.

Yours in style, punctuation, spelling, and grammar
(and the occasional bits of profanity),

SPOGG

ALTERNATIVE PUNCTUATION MARKS (OH, THE IRONY)

*One good thing could come from this horror: it could spell
the end of the age of irony.*

—*ROGER ROSENBLATT, TIME MAGAZINE, SEPTEMBER 2001*

*There's going to be a seismic change. I think it's the end of
the age of irony.*

—*GRAYDON CARTER, EDITOR OF* **VANITY FAIR***, SEPTEMBER 2001*

Shortly after September 11, 2001, mass media pundits declared
irony dead. Six years later, typographers are abuzz over a new
bit of punctuation, called the zing or the snark, among other
things. Depending on whom you talk to, it looks like a disoriented question mark, a pooping inchworm, a Harry Potter scar,
or a curiously decorated nipple. See figure 1:

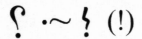

Fɪɢ. 1

It's purpose? To show irony . . .
Irony is dead. Long live irony.

It's not the first time that fans of irony have attempted to recruit punctuation to their cause. In the late 1800s, the French poet Alcanter de Brahm proposed just such a mark. Nothing happened. In 1966, his countryman Hervé Bazin, a writer specializing in teen-angst drama and dysfunctional family relationships, built on the idea. He proposed punctuation to communicate many ideas, including:

doubt (an exclamation point with a question mark's curve at its peak);

certainty (a crossed exclamation point);

authority (an exclamation point with an arrow pointing upward);

indignation (an upside-down exclamation point); and

love (a heart over an exclamation mark's dot).

Of these, only the heart over a dot ever caught on, and its use was restricted to girls in junior high school. Even so, it's worth paying attention to the typographers' zeal. Their ancestors—printers—invented many of our still-functional punctuation marks. These people are the closest thing we have to arbiters of the English alphabet and its accoutrements, and they have in fact sneaked the mark into several typefaces already.

Despite this, SPOGG believes the snark's future is limited. Ditto for *Slate* magazine's "sarcasm point," an inverted exclamation point unsoftened by even a squiggle, a curve, or a teenybopperish heart. Either could possibly join the ranks of the emoticon, those odd little faces made from various punctuation marks and appended into certain types of electronic communication to help clarify the author's intent. The same is true for the interrobang, a question mark/exclamation point hybrid meant to express disbelief.*

This is not the job of punctuation, historically speaking. Remember, we first used it to tell people when to breathe as they read out loud, later using it to help silent readers understand syntax. Punctuation isn't meant to make the author's state of mind clear. Well-chosen words do that, and the day serious writers turn to punctuation to communicate their ideas will be a:-(day, indeed.

YANKEE DOODLE'S DANDY

Where Americans have quotation marks, the British have inverted commas. Where we have periods, the Brits come to a nice, sturdy full stop. The bigger difference between British and American punctuation is where it falls in relation to the quotation marks. Here's how a quote would look in American English:

The president's favorite song is "Fixing a Hole."

Here's how it would look in British style:

The queen's favourite song is "Lucy in the Sky with Diamonds".

Look! The period is on the wrong side of the road! The same goes for question marks, commas, and exclamation points.

---

* Can you believe that Microsoft's new ClearType font collection supports the interrobang!?

They go on the wrong side of the road, unless the quote is a complete sentence, and the sentence ends with it:

He said, "I like both songs." On this, the Americans and British agree.

We should further point out that some British publications, though not the forward-looking BBC, even use a single inverted comma instead of the full set, so you'll have to be focused to impress the queen with your accuracy. Still. There is something to the British way of doing things that we rather like. If you were to adopt their style over ours, it's likely that only a professional editor would bring down the hammer on your head; these punctuation differences don't change the meaning of a sentence. And even though global politics would prevent the queen from telling you she's impressed by your command of British style, deep down, we know she'd be thrilled.

From Courtney Love's online journal entry:
*we were doing our hair (thew girls) way up in that ugly crazy
building and couyld seeyou all for blocks, it was wild.*

6.

No, You Can't Has Cheezburger? The Parts of Speech and How Sentences Form

The Society for the Promotion of Good Grammar

Dear Mr. President:

We at the Society for the Promotion of Good Grammar salute you!

When you recently said, "People that want to be a citizen of this country ought to learn English," your sentiments were music to our ears. It's not that we don't love Spanish. It's a beautiful language. SPOGG exists, however, to promote clear, concise, and accurate English.

This is why, in addition to our salute, we are delivering a bit of a slap. What you should have said was this: "People *who* want to be *citizens* of this country ought to learn English."

If our president is going to expect this much of his

citizens, then we are going to expect the same—and more—from him.

Sincerely yours,

SPOGG

We're still awaiting the president's reply. . . .

Ignorant people think it's the noise which fighting cats make that is so aggravating, but it ain't so; it's the sickening grammar they use.

—MARK TWAIN

Mark Twain had the wrong idea about cat grammar. You can't really blame him, though. He died before we developed data-tracking devices that inform us that every month, 250,000 people with an abundance of spare time visit Web sites whose sole purpose is to display photos of cats with bad grammar.

"I CAN HAS CHEEZBURGER?" is the caption that's launched a thousand imitators. (More than a thousand, actually. A Google search on LOLcats reveals more than three million references to them.) While the cats are cute, especially the fat cheeseburger-eater, it's really the bad grammar that provides that je ne sais quoi that elevates the site from a mere oddity to a cult phenomenon.

For language lovers, the bad grammar is a curious sort of catnip. "I CAN HAS CHEEZBURGER?" contains a spelling blunder, a syntax irregularity, a missing article, and a verb conjugation goof. That's four mistakes in four words—catastrophic from an English teacher's point of view. But to write off the errors as merely bad grammar would be to miss a crucial development in LOLcat evolution. The cats' grammar might be bad, but it's bad in consistent ways. We're creating a whole separate cat grammar using broken bits of our own.

For example, the caption "I ARE SERIOUS CAT" has the wrong verb conjugation and is missing the article—two error types that made "I CAN HAS CHEEZBURGER?" a sensation. "I ARE SERIOUS . . ." might be a spelling error short of being good kitty pidgin, but it shows that even when we're purposely creating humor out of bad grammar, we like it when the mistakes follow certain rules. These rules are established enough that some software geeks have even written an LOLcatese generator for people unable to achieve fluency on their own.

When the rules of LOLcat grammar are broken, the results show it. Consider the caption "MY SON HE HAS A FLAVOR." Even though flavor humor is one of the established categories of the oeuvre, this one just isn't all that funny. It's like the way Yoda impersonations are good only if word order properly messed up is. If it's not, then it's just stupid, which proves that humans are serious about our grammar, even when we're joking

Unless you want to be an inadequate LOLcat, you r know how to form clean, clear sentences. To do this, y to know how words fit together to form meaningf Understanding the parts of speech is key. Just as l building blocks of words, properly assembled gr become phrases and clauses, the building blocks

Unlike puzzle pieces, which can play just on picture, the same word can snap into a varie spots, playing a variety of different roles in "Dog" is one. The slobbery variety might be th of the LOLcat (except the "I HAS A HAT" kitten, who's wearing a hound dog's ear on his head). But "dog" is not only a noun. It can also be a verb that means to follow someone closely. This means we don't have to assign words to categories in the abstract and memorize long lists of them. But we do need to know generally what the categories are, and how they relate to each other. This way, our sentences have a shot at making sense—in English or in LOLcat.

ARTICLES IDENTIFY OBJECTS AND PEOPLE

Articles—"the," "a," and sometimes "an"—accompany nouns. They're everywhere. The most commonly used word in the English language, in fact, is "the." It's a remarkably flexible word, which can be used to identify single objects (the chair) and entire nations of people (the Danish).

Its partner is "a" or "an." The difference between the two can sometimes be subtle. "The" is a definite article, used to identify a particular object or person. "A" is indefinite, to be used when any old chair or nationality will do. Its cousin "an" is the alternative when the article comes before words that start with a vowel, or are pronounced as though they do, like "herb" and "honor."

While this sounds pretty darned clear-cut, things can get ore subtle. In his book *When You Catch an Adjective, Kill It*, the ter Ben Yagoda uses a charming anecdote explaining how happens (as well as the effect of a good editor). Harold a midcentury editor of the *New Yorker*, was apparently bout the difference between "the" and "a." When Vladimir Nabokov submitted a piece describing "the nutcracker" that was passed around, Ross wanted to know if the house contained only one. If so, "the" was the appropriate choice. Apparently Nabokov didn't permit the change when the piece ran in the magazine. But when he included it in his anthology *Speak, Memory*, he used "a." It seems, then, that the Nabokovs were a multinutcracker clan.

"The" and "a" can also be used to indicate prominence—a sometimes arbitrary judgment, but the writer's to make. "The singer Christina Aguilera" is how we refer to someone nationally known for her profession. "Jane Warbler, a singer," is someone who probably needs to hold down a day job.

There can also be a time component to choosing the right article. The first time a writer talks about a kitten using a dog's ear for a hat, the indefinite article is appropriate. The second time, though, it's "the" kitten with the dog-ear hat.

ON NOUNS

We still love Jon Stewart, despite this blunder in a commencement speech he gave in May 2004 at the College of William and Mary.

"We declared war on terror. We declared war on terror—it's not even a noun, so, good luck."

The Noun Is a Person, Place, Thing, or Concept (Including the Aforementioned "Terror")

Linguists, an often grumpy bunch, hate this *Schoolhouse Rock* definition, and would prefer that we categorize words based on their function in our sentences. This is fine for people who've studied linguistics and have the vocabulary to describe such things. For most nouns and most people, "person, place, thing, or concept" works just fine. Mrs. Krebapple, school, apple, terror: it's not that hard to follow.

Other clues help identify nouns when the fog of words thickens. Nouns often appear with articles. They have plural and singular forms, as well as a sort of plural called a "collective" noun, which is a singular noun that refers to a group of people (the family, the team, the band), at least in American English. British English treats these as plurals.

In a sentence, a noun can do all sorts of jobs—it's not restricted to being just the subject or the object. Nouns can also occur in phrases (the cable guy, for example).

The Pronoun Is a Type of Noun That Acts as a Replacement for an Object, a Person, or a Noun Phrase.

Like saccharine and the toupee, noun replacements can be unpleasant.

They can be unclear:

His father died when he was six.

They can be incorrectly chosen:

He gave Jackie and I his Academy Award.

They can also be misspelled:

Its a small world, after all.

Despite this, most pronouns are easy to master. There are the straightforward personal ones: "I," "you," "he," "she," "it," "we," and "they." These are called subjective because they can stand in for the subject of a sentence.

Then there are the objective pronouns, which replace or represent a sentence's object: "me," "him," "her," "it," "us," "them." "Between you and I" is a common abomination ("between" is a preposition, requiring "me" as its object). Otherwise, most people—even if they don't know the boring grammatical terms—know when to use "I" and when to use "me" in all other cases. Exceptions are Cookie Monster, who is a brainless puppet, and 2 Live Crew, who sang the following without terminal mortification: "Me so horny! Me love you long time!"

There are also the possessive pronouns: "mine," "yours," "his," "hers," "its," "ours," and "theirs." Confusing "it's" (it is) with "its" is a common error.*

Here are other pronoun types:

Demonstrative pronouns: Words that show something. "This," "that," "these," and "those." The same words can also function as adjectives, a distinction that matters only for people who enjoy playing "What part of speech is that" during cocktail-party lulls.

Interrogative pronouns: Question words. "Who"? "whom"? "which"? "what"? Also, "whoever"? "whomever"? "whichever"? "whatever"?

Relative pronouns: Like the interrogative ones, but without the question marks. The most common error with these is when people confuse "who" with "that." People get "who"; inanimate objects get "that." There are relaxed types who insist there is no meaningful distinction between "who" and "that." We couldn't disagree more vigorously. We're just guessing here, but we

---

* "Our" and "their" sound like possessive pronouns, but they're not; they act as adjectives.

suspect they might also be unable to tell the difference between a human and a blow-up doll. That must be a nice thing when they need to drive in the carpool lane or occupy themselves on a lonely Saturday night. There are some exceptions. A sentence such as "Who is it that framed Roger Rabbit" sounds better than "Who is it who framed Roger Rabbit?" But "Who framed Roger Rabbit?" is better than either. Don't let squishy prose be an excuse for turning people into things.

Indefinite pronouns: "All," "another," "any," "anybody," "anyone," "anything," "each," and similar words. The trick with these is to match singular pronouns with singular verbs, and plural pronouns with plural verbs. This can be easier said than done. "Everyone" and "everybody" are pretty easy—"one" and "body" are singular.

Intensive and reflexive pronouns: "Myself," "himself," "herself," "itself," "ourselves," "themselves." They can be used for emphasis (intensive), or to refer back to the subject (reflexive). *I, myself, would never do that. I saw myself in the mirror.* Some people are under the mistaken impression that "myself" is simply an elegant variation of plain old "me." This is the equivalent of inserting a silver shrimp fork into your nose. The specialized fork is an elegant thing to be sure, but it's meant for shrimp, not sinuses.

Bush-League Pronoun Problem

Do you have pronoun problems? You're in good company. It's not just President Bush who's plagued. Jane Austen erred in *Pride and Prejudice* when she had Elizabeth Bennet tell Mr. Darcy, "To be sure, you knew no actual good of me—but nobody thinks of that when they [sic] fall in love." This should assuage anyone who's ever mixed up ~~their~~ his or her pronouns.

VERB—A WORD INDICATING AN ACTION OR STATE OF BEING

We're not about to criticize Gertrude Stein's prose. She wrote a memoir in the voice of her lifelong companion, Alice B. Toklas, and it became a bestseller. That doesn't mean that we have to agree with everything she ever said, though. Consider her nutty opinion of the verb:

> Verbs and adverbs are more interesting. In the first place they have one very nice quality and that is that they can be so mistaken. It is wonderful the number of mistakes a verb can make and that is equally true of its adverb.

This is a bit like saying that possums are interesting because they are so often accidentally squashed by cars, and can then be used in many delicious and unexpected recipes. We beg to differ; possums are interesting only because they have prehensile tails and the face of Satan. Meanwhile, verbs are interesting not in their tendency to be mistaken, but for the action and interest they lend sentences.

Regardless of your opinion of verbs, you can't say they're a trivial part of speech. Not too many sentences can stand without them. Seriously! What's more, "verb" comes from *verbum*, the Latin term for "word"—evidence that verbs are the very root of language. They're so important that our next chapter is about them in all their glory. For now, though, remember this.

Verbs change form depending on four factors:

how many people are in on the action;

when the action was performed;

whether the subject of the sentence performed or received the action; and

the "mood" of the sentence, an intimidatingly vague way of saying whether the action has happened, might happen, could happen, or should happen.

From the Perhaps-Gertrude-Stein-Had-a-Point Files: This headline ran in the June 17, 2007, *New York Times*:

Abbas Swears in Emergency Cabinet

An emergency cabinet for cursing, eh? That's a #¥©<!^} good idea.

ADJECTIVES MODIFY NOUNS AND PRONOUNS

Mark Twain called adjectives beasts that should be caught and, for the most part, killed. The radio host Clifton Fadiman called them the "banana peel of the parts of speech." Writers and editors tend to heap similar scorn on adjectives. We get this. Very often, the right noun can carry its own weight. The word "davenport," for example, means a large, well-upholstered sofa. (It's also a city in Iowa, so thank goodness for capital letters or we'd give the impression we liked to sit in corn.)

Adjectives are useful for comparisons. Davenports can be comfortable or lumpy. But they can also be more comfortable and lumpier, or even most comfortable and lumpiest. Adjectives also tell information about color, size, number, and other qualities that pertain to nouns and pronouns. What's really interesting here is that there is a hierarchy of these adjective categories. You wouldn't, for example, call a pair of chairs the "dilapidated two creaky chairs." You'd say, "two creaky, dilapidated chairs."

And while we're on the topic of two creaky, dilapidated chairs, we might as well explain how to tell if a comma should be inserted between a pair of adjectives. If they both modify the noun, and if it doesn't matter which order they go in, stick in a comma. Likewise, if you can substitute an "and" for the comma and the sentence still makes sense, insert the commas. If it doesn't (say, in the case of the movie *The Giddy Old Maid*), then don't use a comma.

An Adverb Modifies a Verb, an Adjective,
Another Adverb, a Phrase, or a Clause.
It Indicates How, When, Where, or How
Much Something Was Done, As Well
As How Often.

Ponder this scene from the movie *Deliverance*, where two spooky men from the mountain contemplate a fresh conquest named Ed, played by a young Ned Beatty.

MOUNTAIN MAN: *What do you want to do now?*
TOOTHLESS MAN [GRINNING]: *He's got a real pretty mouth on him, don't he?*
MOUNTAIN MAN: *Ain't that the truth.*
TOOTHLESS MAN [TO ED]: *You gonna do some prayin' for me, boy. And you better pray real good.*

Some people, when they hear this exchange in *Deliverance*, worry for poor Ed, who's about to be made to squeal like a pig.

Other people, though, can't get past the Toothless Man's inability to use an adverb properly. Anything else that might have happened in that scene is a mere blur because of it. It's a *really* pretty mouth, Mr. Shoulda Flossed.

Dropping an adverb's *-ly* is called flattening it. Even though this happens in speech all the time, it sounds barbaric to anyone who wasn't raised in the woods. It should never happen in writing, unless you're trying to capture the sound of someone who talks like he grew up sleeping on boulders and combing his hair with pinecones.

While we're talking about *-ly*, it's a common misperception that all words that end in *-ly* are adverbs. Some words, such as "friendly," "portly," and "measly," are adjectives that just happen to end in *-ly*. (We suppose they could be made into adverbs—*he greeted the mountain men friendlily*. But we wouldn't recommend it.)

At any rate, the disdain for adverbs is such that the title of the final Harry Potter book, *Harry Potter and the Deathly Hallows*, came under the fire of a wild-eyed, crabby blogger. It's true that J. K. Rowling, especially in the earlier books, couldn't resist buttering her prose with adverbs. Harry and Ron speak to each other quietly, darkly, and even angrily (but oddly, never magically, and certainly not magically deliciously). But in title of the seventh book, "deathly" is an adjective.

In short, don't get so blinded by hatred for a part of speech that you reject anything that looks like it. It's often true that verbs can carry the weight of verb-and-adverb combinations, but it's also true that judiciously used adverbs can work wonders, allowing writers to boldly go where they might have crept before.

HOLLYWOOD FLATTENS ANOTHER ADVERB: A PRIME EXAMPLE

The Society for the Promotion
of Good Grammar

Ms. Stacey Snider
Universal Pictures Chairman—Marketing

Dear Ms. Snider:

The Society for the Promotion of Good Grammar loves Meryl Streep, especially her turn as grammar-obsessed Aunt Josephine in Lemony Snicket's *A Series of Unfortunate Events*. Alas, we have been informed of an unfortunate event of a marketing nature regarding her movie *Prime*.

You were generous to send a box of prime-quality frozen meats to key film critics, one of whom shared the contents with us. The accompanying note describes the film, alarmingly, as "a real juicy romance." If the romance is genuine but literally oozing juice, then you would need a comma separating the words "real" and "juicy." This is often the case when you have a string of adjectives modifying a word.

To investigate whether the movie literally dribbles the juices of Ms. Streep, we visited your Web site, which informed us that *Prime* was "a gentle comedy that weaves a tale of two lovers trying to keep the flame alive as an unusual obstacle is hurled in their path."

We suspect the unusual obstacle is metaphorical, and not, say, the box of frozen steaks and hamburger patties that we wish we had received ourselves.

We conclude, then, that the movie is merely metaphorically juicy, and we would recommend all further meat deliveries be accompanied with a note that describes *Prime* as a "really juicy" romance.

With that small change, your meat recipients can anticipate the joys of their meat and movie with all the appropriate forms of salivation, and none of the horror of unclear grammar.

Sincerely yours,

SPOGG

CONJUNCTIONS LINK WORDS, PHRASES, AND CLAUSES

Conjuctions come in three varieties:

Coordinating: "and," "but," "or," "nor," "for," "so," and "yet." These link words (dog and cat), phrases (the dog and cat), and independent clauses (the dog ate the cat, and the cat objected strenuously).

Subordinating: When a clause is dependent on another, a subordinating conjunction introduces it (as this very sentence demonstrates). The most common subordinating conjunctions are "after," "although," "as," "because," "before," "how," "if," "once," "since," "than," "that," "though," "till," "until," "when," "where," "whether," "and" "while."

Correlative conjunctions: Like adolescent girls in the bathroom, these work in pairs. Unlike adolescent girls, they don't switch best friends all the time. They are "both / and"; "either / or"; "neither / nor"; "not only / but also"; "so / as"; and "whether / or".

PREPOSITIONS JOIN NOUNS, PRONOUNS, AND PHRASES TO OTHER WORDS IN A SENTENCE. THE NOUN, PRONOUN, OR PHRASE IS THE OBJECT OF THE PREPOSITION.

If the preposition were an animal, it would be a black cat, tarred senselessly with superstition. Many an English teacher has said we must not use them to end our sentences. But those fusspots aren't worth listening to. Nor is the subject worth talking about. And there you have two sentences that demonstrate why this preposition proclamation is a silly one, foisted upon us by people who wish English were just like Latin. As long as the sentence flows naturally, it can end with a preposition. It's preferable, in fact, to primly tangled syntax. Imagine if Bonnie Raitt had called her song "Something About Which to Talk." That's something to which no one would have wanted to listen. It's also preferable to the sort of thing that can happen when one tries to be hypercorrect, as Paul McCartney did in "Live and Let Die." He wrote, "But in this ever-changing world in which we live **in** [*sic*] makes you give in and cry, just live and let die." It's not the world that's doing it, Sir Paul, just some of the songwriters.*

Another common problem occurs when people fail to match their prepositions with their verbs. No one objected to the catchphrases "war on terror" and "war on Christmas." Now, the *Washington Post* copy editor who wrote a headline that said PRESIDENT DEFENDS WAR ON JULY 4TH is paying the price. Who can read that without thinking that patriotism is under assault, and our own president is leading the troops?

Against, people. The war against terror. That's the preposition you can't refuse.

Here are other common verb-preposition pairs worth studying:

account for
admit to
agree with
apologize for
appeal to
approve of
argue with / about
arrange for
ask for
base on
beg for
begin with

---

* Note: Some people give Sir Paul the benefit of the doubt and say the lyric is actually "this . . . world in which we're livin'." We believe the experiment known as Wings removes the benefit of the doubt from Sir Paul forever.

believe in

belong to

benefit from

boast about (And brag about—not brag on. Never, ever. Noooo.)

bring to

care for / about

cater to

choose between

compare with / to ("with" emphasizes similarities; "to" emphasizes differences)

concern about / with

congratulate on

consist of

despair of

differ from

distinguish somebody / something from / between somebody / something

dream of / about

elaborate on

escape from (Never mind the movie *Escape to Witch Mountain*. All sorts of weird and unfortunate things happened in the seventies. See *Deliverance*.)

fight against / with / for

guess at

hear of / about

hope of / for

mistake for

pray for

react against / to

succeed in
take from
think of / about
wait for (not wait on, unless you're hoping for tips)

INTERJECTIONS—EXCLAMATIONS USED FOR EMPHASIS, OFTEN WITH AN EXCLAMATION POINT.

Technically, interjections don't have a grammatical function, but they're fun. And how! Here are more:

Yes!
Alas!
Rats!
How rude!
As if!
Crikey!
Fine!

PUTTING THEM ALL TOGETHER

Parts of speech come together to form phrases and clauses. A phrase is a group of words that are related grammatically, but don't have both a subject and a predicate. It's a part of a sentence, and not the whole thing.

A clause, meanwhile, has both subject and predicate, and can stand alone as a sentence. Clauses can also be linked by conjunctions or semicolons.

This is a phrase: *Monty Python and the Holy Grail*

This is a clause: *The Empire Strikes Back*

Here's that same clause with the subject in bold and the predicate underlined:

The Empire <u>strikes back.</u> ("The" is an article identifying the "Empire," and "back" is an adverb modifying "strikes.")

Here are two clauses linked with a conjunction (and an interjection):

The Empire strikes back, and Luke loses a hand. Gross!

Sentences can get more complex, with compound subjects and compound verbs. **The Wookies and Ewoks** <u>fall in love</u> *and, despite huge size differences,* <u>breed offspring.</u>

Sentences can also have implied subjects. These are called imperatives. For example:

Die hard!

The implied subject is *you.*

FOUR BIG THINGS THAT CAN GO WRONG WITH SENTENCES

1. Misplaced Modifiers

Assembling simple sentences is straightforward. People who can form even simple ones can go on to achieve great things in life, if not in their communication. So what if they're a bit dull? At least they're safe.

It's when we start dressing things up with modifiers that we get ourselves into trouble. Take the song "I Only Have Eyes for You." It's a lovely sentiment that the Flamingos intended. But what they meant to say was "I Have Eyes for You Only." That sentence means, "I don't want to look at anybody other than you." As they sang it, though, the song means, "I have eyeballs for you, but you can forget about chocolates, roses, and especially real estate. I'm rolling in eyes, baby. Hope that's not grossing you out."

The misplaced-modifier problem can get worse. In the movie *Animal Crackers*, Groucho Marx shows us how:

"One morning, I shot an elephant in my pajamas. How he got into my pajamas, I'll never know."

So, as you assemble your phrases and clauses, and dress them up with detail, make sure you place your modifier near the word or phrase it's supposed to enrich. That way, you'll never write a sentence like this headline, which appeared on a major Internet portal:

Man Smuggles Monkey onto Airplane in His Hat

That must have been one heck of a hat. Or one very tiny airplane, and even more minuscule monkey.

2. Run-on Sentences/Comma Splices

It's easy, when reviewing the online ramblings of Courtney Love, to find problems. To wit:

We were doing our hair(thew girls) way up in that ugly crazy building and couyld seeyou all for blocks, it was wild.

The challenge is to make enough sense of her writing to find the actual words, and from there, to determine where the major errors lie. This is how her online journal entry reads after the Basic Literacy Scrub, a form of detoxification for drug-addled celebrity screeds:

We were doing our hair (the girls) way up in that ugly crazy building and could see you all for blocks, it was wild.

Now, the sentence makes a primitive sort of sense. As we read it, Courtney Love and friends were doing their hair in a room on one of the upper floors of an ugly building. They could see her fans for blocks. It was wild.

She needed to break that crazy ramble into at least two, if not three, sentences. The "it was wild" portion after the comma is a comma splice. Comma splices occur when two complete (if drunk and/or high) sentences are joined with a comma. They should either be joined by a semicolon, or separated by a period or exclamation point. *We could see you all for blocks; it was wild!*

It is true that sometimes, comma splices aren't grammatically incorrect. Really simple sentences can be joined by commas (*She's not a porn star, she's a rock star*). But some people will object even to that. So, avoid comma splices, lest you end up sounding every bit as coherent as poor Courtney Love. Which is to say, not at all.

3. Confounding Pronouns

Pronouns save time. It's much easier to say, "Dr. Hassenfeffer made some of his signature brownies" than Dr. Hassenfeffer made some of "Dr. Hassenfeffer's signature brownies." What's more, they're easier on the brain. Researchers using MRI machines found that proper names lit up a part of the brain not normally linked with language—the parietal lobe, which is used to process spatial images. The researchers, writing in the journal *NeuroReport*, concluded that the brain was making a picture of the person whose proper name was used. Every time the proper name was used, that portion of the subject's brain went to work. This doesn't happen with pronouns, making them easier on the brain. As with any shortcut, though, there are wolves looking to take advantage of your would-be Red Riding Hoods. Look what happened to poor Chloe Sevigny in the pages of *US Weekly*:

> I shaved my head when I was 17. I sold it for $500 to a famous Broadway wigmaker.

She meant to say she had sold her *hair*. But she should have mentioned that little detail, using "hair" as an antecedent. *I shaved off my hair when I was 17. I sold it for $500.* Any time there is a pronoun, we look to the noun that comes before it—the antecedent—to understand its meaning. Take care that yours matches.

Some people get really fussy with antecedents. Not long ago, there was considerable debate over an SAT question that said, "Toni Morrison's genius enables her to create novels that arise from and express the injustices African Americans have endured." Students were supposed to identify the grammatical error in the sentence; the test's authors maintained there were none. Some people claimed the "her" was inappropriate because "Toni Morrison's" is part of the noun phrase "Toni Morrison's genius" and is therefore not a proper antecedent. SPOGG believes this is fussiness gone too far. The sentence is clear and unambiguous, and that, after all, is our goal.

4. Subject-Verb Disagreement

Jack Nicholson was completely disagreeable when he said

this to *In Touch Weekly*: "There's only two people in the world you should lie to: the police and your girlfriend."

We're not talking about the lies, of course. We're talking about "There's only two . . ." There is only two? There is two? No, Jack. There *are* only two. That takes care of the first error, and would probably take care of the second, but just in case Jack doesn't know the difference between a collective noun and a regular one, we're going to tell him.

In this instance, "police" takes the plural. In American English, collective nouns do sometimes take the singular. When members of the collective act independently, the word takes a plural. When they act together, they take a singular. So, "The class finished its project" (a group effort), but "The class finished their exams" (each person took one test).

What Jack should have said is this: "The police and your girlfriend are the only people in the world you should lie to."

Did he learn nothing from *The Witches of Eastwick*?

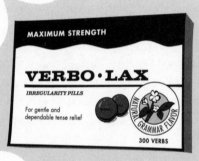

7.

Things That Make Us Tense

**The Society for the Promotion
of Good Grammar**

Dear Rick Moranis:

The Society for the Promotion of Good Grammar is a big fan of your work. We loved your performance in *My Blue Heaven*. You made a fine Holly in *Miss Spider's Sunny Patch Kids*. And don't even get us started on the wonder that is *Ghostbusters*.

We do, however, have some concerns about your legacy, specifically because of your film *Honey, I Shrunk the Kids*. It should have been, *Honey, I've Shrunk the Kids* or *Honey, I Shrank the Kids*. We understand the producers thought "shrunk" sounded funnier, but to us, bad grammar is no laughing matter.

Now that you have moved on to a country-music career, we urge you to become a grammatically correct cowboy. You can't make the past perfect, but there's no need to make the present tense.

You know you want to be good. You already sing this, after all:

> *I ain't from nowhere near Kentucky.*
> *No right to sing them southern blues.*
> *I'm from Toronto, snowy city,*
> *From a neighbourhood of Jews.*

You're Canadian, Mr. Moranis. You grew up with Jews, and we know from being married to one (who grew up near Kentucky, actually) that they're a bookish people. It would be so easy, too; all you'd have to do is sing, "I'm not from near Kentucky/I've no right to sing the southern blues. . . ."

Think of it. You could be the Grammatical Canadian Cowboy, the first and probably last of your kind. Isn't that what every cowboy really wants?

Sincerely yours,

SPOGG

P.S. Are you a Maple Leafs fan? If so, please let them know that it's Maple Leaves. LEAVES.

P.P.S. Also, in the United States, "neighborhood" is the preferred spelling.

> *In the Big Rock Candy Mountains, the jails are made of tin*
> *And you can walk right out again as soon as you are in*
> *There ain't no short-handled shovels, no axes saws or picks*
> *I'm a goin' to stay where you sleep all day,*

Where they ~~hung~~ hanged the jerk ~~that~~ who invented work
In the Big Rock Candy Mountains
[spogg ~~wuz~~ was here]

They might not care about verbs in the Big Rock Candy Mountains, but we're not living there, and the jerk who invented work hasn't been hanged; he's expecting us to show up at 8 a.m. sharp on Saturday for inventory at the garter-belt factory.

Nouns are a snap. Jails, shovels, axes, picks . . . these are not complicated things. There aren't past-tense, present-tense, and future-tense jerks. Nor are nouns subject to confounding moods, something that afflicts both verbs and human beings. And speaking of shared woes, consider the problem of irregularity. In humans, it's an unspeakable condition best prevented by healthy fiber intake. In verbs, irregularity is worse, even if the results are sometimes comical.

But let's go back to "hang" and "hanged," shall we? The past tense of "hang" is "hung" when it's an object being suspended. *He hung the painting in the attic.* When it's a person, though, it's "hanged"—at least when death is on the line. *The criminal was hung* means something else entirely, something that's neither your business nor ours, and impossible to tell anyway due to the loose fit of prison-issued pants. While there are those who argue that "hung" can be used in all contexts, this is a terrible idea for two reasons. You might be misinterpreted and some people will think you're a pervert, or they might just think you're a rube for not knowing which verb form to use. Pervert or rube: you can do better with your reputation.

Fortunately, hanging is the preferred method of execution in only two states, and that's only if the dead man walking chooses that over lethal injection. So, as a grammatical error, its frequency is increasingly rare. This is alas not the case when it comes to errors in pop culture. When an incorrect verb form makes it into a movie title, for example, we're likely to have to tolerate it again in the sequel, and later on TV when one of the low-budget channels decides to turn it into a weekly series. Enough!

REGULAR VERSUS IRREGULAR: WHAT'S THE DIFFERENCE?

Once upon a time, and not that long ago, verbs were either weak or strong. The weak verbs stayed the course. They didn't change their vowels to make past tense and past participles. The strong ones did (which means their original vowels would cut and run). Understandably, people were flummoxed by these so-called strong and weak behaviors. Now we call verbs regular and irregular. Regular ones—the bulk—add a -d or -ed to make the past tense and past participles. *I walk; I walked; I have walked.* Irregular verbs, of which there are about three hundred, change in various ways to make their past and perfect forms. *I run, I ran, I've run.*

Many of these are such common verbs that we native speakers just know them. There are three, though, that can befuddle even the most confident writers and speakers.

Lay and Lie

We hate to pick on Bob Dylan. He's one of the greatest song-writers of the twentieth century, but unless his song "Lay, Lady, Lay" was about a chicken, he set the cause of verb conjugation back quite a bit. We'd like to give him the benefit of the doubt, and consider it an example of poultry emotion, but that raises an equally disturbing set of concerns. Here's what he sings:

Lay, lady, lay, lay across my big brass bed
Lay, lady, lay, lay across my big brass bed
Whatever colors you have in your mind
I'll show them to you and you'll see them shine

In his defense, he probably didn't want to encourage his ladylove to tell untruths. Nor did he wish to compromise his ability to get laid by impugning her veracity. After all, "lie" and "lie" sound and are spelled the same. But in the present tense, which is how we describe action taking place now, "lay" is correct only if it takes an object. You can lay yourself down to sleep. You can lay an egg (assuming you're that sort of animal). But you can't just *lay*.

Here's how both verbs appear in the various tenses:

Lie
Present: I lie down for a nap every day after lunch.
Past: I lay down for my afternoon nap, and didn't wake up until the next morning.
Past participle: I have lain in this bed for hours, and still can't sleep.
Present participle: I am lying in bed, dreaming of chickens.

Lay:
Present: Lay, lady, lay! I need eggs!
Past: Exasperated, Bob laid his Barbie on the table.

Past participle: The chicken refused, so Bob has laid an egg himself.

Present participle: Ken is laying out a picnic of egg salad on rye for Barbie.

Rise and Raise

Like "lie" "and" "lay," "rise" and "raise" sound similar, and both have to do with upward motion. Raise requires an object, though, and "rise" doesn't. Raise your hand (an object!) if you think you can remember this.

Rise:

rise, rose, risen, rising

Present: We rise at dawn.

Past: We rose with the sun.

Past participle: I have risen to face my enemies.

Raise:

raise, raised, raising, raising

Present: I raise my hand and salute you.

Past: They raised Buffy from the dead, and she resented it.

Past participle: We were raising corn, but some children ruined the crop while worshipping a malevolent deity.

Note: to raise or to rear?

Some insist "rearing" is the only verb you can use when talking about the work of raising children. "Rearing" is a fine word, and we do get a sort of effervescent thrill of popping very specific and correct words into sentences. In the United States, though, it's common to use "raise" with crops and children (and the dead)—common enough that it's probably no longer wrong. Still, no one will fault you if you continue to rear your offspring.

Sit and Set

While the idea of settin' on the porch drinkin' moonshine sounds appealing, it's really only something you can say if you're wearing overalls and chewing on a giant plug of tobacky. If that's the case, you can pretty much say anything and we'll slink right back to our cars and drive off, lest you start complimenting our (really) purty mouth. Otherwise, "sit" and "set" is another transitive/intransitive pair. People sit; objects are set.

Sit

Present: He sits at the head of the table.

Past: She sat on an elephant.

Past participle: We were sitting comfortably until some yokel shot the porch swing out from under us.

Set:

Present: I set the gun on the table and look him straight in the eye.

Past: I set my false teeth in a glass last night, but when I woke up, they were gone.

Past participle: We were setting the table when the phone rang.

A Brief List of Irregular Verbs

There are nearly three hundred irregular verbs in English. Here are a few common ones, with strict instructions on their proper use. We're providing the three main tenses in English:

present, past, and perfect. Don't let the term "tense" make you feel tense, though. It simply refers to the time the action takes place. Language experts also sometimes talk about "aspect," and by this, they mean whether an action is completed, repeated, or ongoing ("I am eating" versus "I have eaten"). Tense can get more complicated with sentences such as "We had been talking," but the verb conjugations don't change when they're stacked up like this, and honestly, if you want to read about such particular things as the present and past progressive, there are other books out there. The present, past, and perfect are plenty for now.

To be
Present: I am, you are, he/she/it is, we are, they are
Past: I was, you were, he/she/it was, we were, they were
Participle: add "been." So, I have been, you have been, etc.

The phrase "I been," as in the book called *I Been in Sorrow's Kitchen and Licked Out All the Pots*, is correctly used only by artists and writers aping the grammar of the downtrodden. Bob Dylan did this in 1992 with his album *Good As I Been to You*. If you're actually a member of the downtrodden, say, "I've been," and you're one step closer to having the sort of life that's so pleasant, it will be too boring to write about.

To break
"Broke" has been slang for penniless for hundreds of years. "I'm broke" is a grammatical, if sad, lament. Alas, this expression cannot be used on objects. "My arm is broke" makes you sound like the sort of person who'd be in one of Oprah's down-and-out book choices. There are better ways to get on the show. In any

case, it's break, broke, and broken. I break bread; I broke bread; I've broken bread. Anything else, and you're breaking the rules.

To bring

Neil Diamond commits a serious crime in the name of rhyme in "Play Me." It's serious enough that we've stopped bringing him flowers. The lyrics:

> *Song she sang to me*
> *Song she **brang** to me*
> *Words that rang in me,*
> *Rhyme that sprang from me*

The past tense of bring is brought. Not brang. This is a word used often enough that it's deemed "nonstandard" in the dictionary. Nonstandard is a polite way of saying, "You're using it incorrectly, idiot." There is an exemption if you're Scottish, because there, it is the correct past tense. If you're not wearing a kilt, though, it's not recommended. What's more, the participle is also brought, not broughten—not even if you're Paris Hilton and above most other laws. A message allegedly from Hilton to Lindsay Lohan's allegedly hacked sidekick read as follows: "yes [*sic*] im [*sic*] not denying that [*sic*] but we do not talk on a regular basis, atleast [*sic*] not enough for your name to even be broughten [*sic*] up."

To buy

It's buy, bought, and bought. Not boughten. And not store-boughten. Only children can get away with using a word that the *Columbia Guide to Standard American English* calls "curious," "non-standard," and "dialectical." This error is more likely to be made in northern states, so take heart, southerners. You don't have the monopoly on bad usage.

To drink

It's drink, drank, drunk. If you say "I drunk," people will suspect that's not water in your thermos.

To fall

It's fall, fell, fallen. "Felled" is another word entirely. It's the past tense of "fell," which means to cut or knock down. He felled the tree, which felt nothing.

To feel

Speaking of feeling, it's feel, felt, and felt. The knock-knock joke, though amusing, gets it wrong. Knock-knock. Who's there? Chesterfield. Chesterfield who? Chester feeled my leg so I slapped him.

To get

I get it; I got it; and either I've gotten it, or I've got it. In American English, the participle depends on what you'd like to convey. "I've gotten it" means you've recently acquired it. "I've gotten up" means "I've stood," while "I've gotten familiar" with something means "I've become familiar" with it. "I've got it" means it's been in your possession awhile (as opposed to being a recent acquisition). It can also mean you believe you can catch that fly ball soaring over left field. Or, you might say "I've got to have it" when you must possess something. British English generally sticks with just plain "got."

Many people object to got and gotten as ungrammatical, barbaric, or overused. "I've got" can usually be replaced with "I have," which generates no such objections. We suspect the hard *g* and *t* make this word appealing choices in speech. The AOL slogan (and Tom Hanks movie) "You've got mail" is so much perkier than "You have mail." So was the "Got milk?" ad campaign, which was so effective that at one point, nine out of ten Americans had heard it—pretty much guaranteeing the expression is now part of standard English.

To give

It's give, gave, and given. "Gift" has been used as a verb meaning to give for hundreds of years, but we don't like it. There is a perfectly good word already for that thing we do with presents—one that doesn't also mean talented, as "gifted" does. What's more, the sort of people who use "gift" instead of "give" are usually trying to sell you something fancy and unnecessary: a three-stone anniversary band; a silver-plated beer cozy; monthly deliveries of fruit you could just buy at the grocery store.

To go

I go. I went. I've gone. Never "I've went . . ." The rapper Eminem says, "I've went to jail for this woman," meaning his ex-wife, whom he's divorced twice. Clearly, he's a slow learner, and unless you want to be in his class, you'll avoid this barbarism.

To lead

I lead, I led, I've led. Only in its present-tense form does it contain the *a*. It's a tricky one to remember because "led" rhymes with the metal lead—as in the sort of pipe Miss Scarlet used on Professor Plum in the Conservatory. Just remember: She led Fred to bed.

To see

I see, I saw, I've seen. Not "I seen."

To shake

I shake, I shook, I've shaken. Only Elvis and his imperson-ators can say, "I'm all shook up," and this only works grammati-cally because he's clearly so disturbed by the monstrous powers of love that he can't possibly conjugate his verbs correctly. (Legend has it that the song's inspiration was more humble. Otis Blackwell wrote it after a colleague came to him, shook a bottle of soda, and said, "Why don't you write a song called 'All Shook Up'?")

To shine

"Shine" means two things—to emit light, or to polish. The conjugation changes, depending on the meaning. I shine the flashlight; I shone the flashlight; I've shone the flashlight. I shine my shoes; I shined my shoes; I've shined my shoes.

To sing

I sing, I sang, I've sung. Once again Bob Dylan gives us a good example of what not to do. In one of his songs, he sings: "I met this fellow with sunglasses on, / He told me he sung folksongs— / I believed him 'cause he was wearin' sunglasses." (1) Never believe anyone in sunglasses; (2) it should be "he sang" folksongs.

To spring

I spring, I sprang, I've sprung. Sir Mix-A-Lot had it right when he said, "You get sprung," in "Baby Got Back," though we're not really sure what he meant by it. Still, it shows how you can use "get" plus a particle to show you've become or grown into something.

To steal

I steal; I stole; I've stolen. Unless you're speaking LOLcat, in which case, you say, "You stoled ma bucket?" An episode of the cartoon *The PJs* was called "How the Super Stoled Christmas." Its keywords on the Internet Movie Database include "malt liquor," "crack head," and "stupidity." We'll let you draw your own conclusions.

To swing

I swing, I swung, I've swung. And if that's the case, good for you.

To take

I take, I took, I've taken. In case you were wondering whether grade inflation exists, review this question posed by an alleged honor student to the Yahoo! Answers board. It contains a fine demonstration of the hideousness that is "tooken" in the wild.

What classes should be **tooken** [*sic*] by [*sic*] my HighSchool [*sic*] Years 9–12 if I want to be a Plastic Or [*sic*] Pioneering Heart Surgeon? I am in the National Jr. Hornor [*sic*] Society [*sic*] my [*sic*] gpa is 4.5 and i [*sic*] am interested in attending Harvard University.

To think

I think, I thought, I've thought. Therefore, I am.

To throw

I throw, I threw, I've thrown. Up, down, in, out: throw is a handy verb. "Throwed," however, is never an acceptable construction. On a Web site for lawyers representing construction workers, we found this appalling paragraph:

> Stu did something he never had to do before: He recorded a mechanic's lien and gave a stop notice to the construction lender. Stu started getting legal bills monthly and paying out big money. He sued. Nick countersued. It was a race to the courthouse! Winning this lawsuit had become the most important thing in Stu's life. He'd been **throwed** [*sic*] off a job! No matter what the cost, he had to prove it was not his fault, and he had to prove it in court.

Unfortunately, he had to prove it with idiotic lawyers. Poor Stu.

FEELING MOODY?

There are three verb "moods." The most common is the indicative mood, which is used to state a fact or ask a question. For example: *He runs. Is he fast?*

Then there's the imperative mood, which is what we use when we're feeling bossy. *March forth! Give Mama some sugar! Eat your beans!* Very often, the subject of imperative sentences is understood, as opposed to being explicitly stated. When it is in there, it's for emphasis. *You with the plaid pants—freeze!*

The trickiest is the subjunctive mood, which you use when you're talking about something that's not actually true, but you wish it were. *I wish I were a millionaire. I wish I had perfect eyesight. I wish I'd bought stock in eBay.*

PASSIVE VOICE: WHEN IT SHOULD BE AVOIDED BY YOU

Eschew passive voice. An English teacher told us that on the first day of high school, and we were—to use the passive voice—perplexed. First, we had to look up the word "eschew." (It means avoid.) Then we had to look up the definition of the passive voice. Even though it sounds like something quiet and perhaps lispy, it really refers to sentences where the action is performed on the subject, instead of by the subject.

There are a couple of problems with the passive construction. First, it's wordy. *The cake was baked with love by my mother* is much longer than *My mother baked the cake with love.* The second problem is that you don't always know who's performing the action. *The cake was eaten in secret.* Who stole (not "stoled") and ate our cake? The author isn't saying, the weasel. Sometimes, though, it doesn't matter who did it. *The cake thief was arrested.* We can assume the police cuffed the thief (though we'd make a citizen's arrest for such an offense, if we could).

So, to paraphrase our English teacher: Write in the active voice. The passive voice is okay if the person performing the action is secondary.

POSTSCRIPT: YOUR TAX DOLLARS AND VERBS

While studying verbs, we encountered a little gift from the federal government. And by gift, we mean freaky propaganda campaign in which some federal agent has trademarked the word "verb" and coined another, "yellowball," to get our kids exercising. We quote, verbatim:

> VERB™ It's what you do. is a national, multicultural, social marketing campaign* coordinated by the U.S. Department of Health and Human Services' Centers for Disease Control and Prevention (CDC).
>
> *Social marketing campaigns apply commercial marketing strategies to influence the voluntary behavior of target audiences to improve personal and social welfare.

Even more choice language from the VERB™ campaign:

> Nothing replaces the rush and exhilaration of physical activity. Yellowball ignites desire for physical activity freeing kids to play out their dreams—I can't NOT play!

We recognize that obesity is a serious health problem. We don't, however, believe that randomly distributed yellow rubber balls, trademarked parts of speech, and improperly inserted periods are the solution. We're just guessing here, but funding and time set aside for daily gym classes would be a bit more effective.

Nonetheless, as long as we're trademarking parts of speech, here are our ideas for other badly needed social programs:

Colon™. It's what you probe. is a national, multicultural, social marketing campaign* coordinated by the U.S. Department of Health and Human Services' Centers for Disease Control and Prevention (CDC) to get more adults to have colonoscopies. (Partner program is Semicolon™. It's what you're left with if you don't get scoped in time.)

Comma™. It's when you pause. is a national, multicultural, social marketing campaign* coordinated by the U.S. Department of Health and Human Services' Centers for Disease Control and Prevention (CDC) to encourage drivers to slow down at unrestricted intersections.

Period™. It's what you miss. is a national, multicultural, social marketing campaign* coordinated by the U.S. Department of Health and Human Services' Centers for Disease Control and Prevention (CDC) to encourage contraceptive use by sexually active teenagers. Wait, no, scratch that. Abstinence-only education has been proven to be a more ineffective way to spend tax dollars.

8.

Clichés–Why Shakespeare Is a Pox upon Us

The Society for the Promotion of Good Grammar

Adam Schein

Columnist, Fox Sports

Dear Mr. Schein,

We are the Society for the Promotion of Good Grammar, writing to give you the verbal equivalent of a penalty flag. Sports cliché week is over, Mr. Schein. But you're still using clichés like, well, nobody's business.

SPOGG has followed your work for months, hoping against hope that you'd clean up your act. Alas, that has not happened.

What follows is the top portion of your most recent story. All clichés are in capital letters so that you will be able to see them, in case you left your binoculars at the bottom of the barrel, in your back pocket, or perhaps where the sun don't shine.

And we quote:

Terrell Owens' ability to fit in with the Cowboys should be an interesting STORY TO FOLLOW.

In interviewing Owens this week, I am even more convinced that the receiver is clueless and won't change a bit.

During the 20-minute conversation, Owens took no accountability for his actions in Philadelphia, continuously blamed the media [*SPOGG hopes, for the sake of his vocal chords, that you mean continually*], his old agent David Joseph, and Donovan McNabb FOR EVERYTHING UNDER THE SUN, and HAD THE NERVE TO ACTUALLY SAY Drew Rosenhaus never discussed his contract in public.

And it was made CRYSTAL CLEAR that this was a Jerry Jones transaction.

ALL EYES WILL BE ON Owens' attitude; his rapport with the disciplinarian that is Parcells; his connection with Drew Bledsoe; his demand for the football; and his relationships with coaches and players.

In essence, EVERYTHING THAT WENT SOUR for Owens in Philadelphia.

And the Tuna cannot be happy that he will be PEPPERED with questions early in camp about Owens' new book. [*SPOGG wonders: Would the tuna prefer lemon juice and perhaps a sprig of dill?*]

Every conversation, fist-bump, high five,

etc., between Owens, Parcells and Bledsoe will be shown on the highlight shows and ANALYZED TO DEATH. And with all three pretty headstrong, this is going to be a daily show.

Athletes have an excuse for using clichés, Mr. Schein. Their skills are physical. Sportswriters, meanwhile, are supposed to be word jocks. This means less whiffing and more verbal home runs from the likes of you.

How about it? Can you raise the bar? Start giving 110 percent? Wipe the slate clean of clichés? Otherwise, we're going to have to start reading that Schatz guy you work with, when we'd much prefer Scheinola.

Sincerely yours,

SPOGG

From Adam Schein, via e-mail:

Dear SPOGG. Great mail!

FROM *BULL DURHAM*

CRASH: *It's time you started working on your interviews.*
NUKE: *What do I gotta do?*
CRASH: *Learn your clichés. Study them. Know them. They're your friends.*

In *Bull Durham*, Kevin Costner's character, Crash Davis, gives Nuke LaLoosh pretty good advice—at least in the context of the movie. But in the real world, Tim Robbins, who played Nuke, got the girl. Let that be a lesson to people who fraternize with clichés. And by "people," we mean the Fox Sports columnist Adam Schein. Even if he replies to letters, he'll never get his own Susan Sarandon unless he stops stuffing his prose with chestnuts.

IN DEFENSE OF THE CLICHÉ

No one ever gives a surgeon a hard time for choosing a familiar tool to slice open skin. Why not sharpened beaver teeth, or bits of broken mirror? Because, the good doctor might say, the scalpel *works*. Likewise, no one suggests a carpenter pound away at a nail with a river rock or a bleached cow skull. The hammer gets the job done; if the carpenter uses it well, he's considered a craftsman. Wordsmiths might not have to smash thumbs or touch blood to earn a paycheck, but they get nothing but scorn when they reach for a familiar set of tools.

In the world of words, these well-handled hammers and scalpels are known as clichés. The bias against them makes a writer's job more difficult. But the real victim isn't the hack with carpal tunnel syndrome and hemorrhoids. The real victim, alas, is the cliché. Unlike murderers and corrupt businessmen, clichés have no defenders. These once-vaunted phrases are spat upon in high school English classrooms and writer's guides. Newspapers and magazines regularly drench them with bile, invariably criticizing clichés using clichés. *Avoid them at all costs! Like the plague!* The first time a writer did this, it might have been funny. The millionth time? Come on! We believe that would be called . . . a cliché.

The Society for the Promotion of Good Grammar would like to say a word in defense of familiar phrases. A good cliché is succinct. It often communicates something profound or complicated, and nonetheless, is immediately understood. In just four words, "he broke my heart" communicates oceans of sorrow that any postpubescent person can understand. When decent folk hear of heartbreak, they know to console—not call for wrinkle-free metaphors.

If we take language seriously at all, then we need to stop picking on expressions that help us understand each other so well, so quickly. You don't throw out blue jeans because they're broken in. Perhaps you do not wear them to a funeral or job interview, or even with high heels. (Please.) Instead, you love them all the more for the comfort they provide, slipping them on when you need to, and when you can get away with it.

WHEN TO AVOID A CLICHÉ

If you are a writer—of books, of songs, of sports stories—there is almost never time a cliché will serve you well. Gone are the days when writers proudly borrowed from each other's work. Nowadays, what's new is prized. This makes a certain amount of sense. Think of the disappointment you feel when you're at the movies, and you figure out the ending five minutes after the film has begun. You start to notice the uncomfortable seats, the stale popcorn, and the robust aroma of the man behind you.

This is what it's like to read clichés instead of original phrases. Enough of them stacked together become inadvertently funny, like the kissing scenes in *Star Wars Episode II—Attack of the Clones.* Good writers do not send in the clones. But ay, there's the rub: clichés are hard to avoid.

We can blame Shakespeare, who not only penned "ay, there's the rub," but also "eye-sore," "foregone conclusion," "come full circle," "come what may," "bated breath," and even "done to death." And to "give the devil his due," he came up with that one, as well. Shakespeare put in print so many new words and memorable expressions, it's as though he thoroughly squeezed the lemon of our language, leaving us with pith—but not, alas, the kind that writers crave.

Unlike in speech, where clichés tend to evaporate behind hand gestures and attractive hairstyles (yes, we're talking about *you*, television news anchors), the written word leaves hackneyed word choices on permanent display, looking every bit as freakish as the Britney Spears effigy in Madame Tussaud's wax museum. The cliché, like the heaving bosom action of the waxy Spears, neither persuades nor delights. It merely disappoints.

Like an animated pair of wax breasts, clichés add bulk but no meaning to your prose. Why say "this day and age" or "at this time" when you can simply say "now" or "today"? This is where it's helpful to tune your ear. Review the list of bad clichés (page 197). Then rewrite accordingly.

WHEN TO USE A CLICHÉ

A friend of the Society who writes scripts for television sitcoms once proposed an autobiographical comedy. When he pitched it, it was called "The Untitled [Eponymous] Project." Though it sounded exotic to us at the time, apparently this isn't all that unusual. The "Untitled Shonda Rhimes Project," for example, became *Grey's Anatomy*. Yes, that's a bad pun, but it also indicates the show is medically inclined (and possibly even anatomically alluring).

Months later, after the pilot for our friend's show was ordered, his creation still didn't have a name. He asked for suggestions, so we sent a few pun-based ideas along. In our defense, it was almost lunchtime and we don't do our best thinking when we're hungry.

Our friend, to our chagrin, sent no reply. We feared we'd insulted him, but that was before we learned about the "Untitled Shonda Rhimes Project." We were totally Hollywood without even knowing it.

When we heard the final name of our friend's show—*It's News to Me*—a little part of our heart turned to glass and shattered. The title was not a pun; it was worse—a cliché. His entire life had been reduced to a single, pat phrase. Apparently, though, this works with the Nielsen families. Well enough that it's given us an idea. Several, actually . . .

The Society for the Promotion
of Good Grammar

Dear Hollywood,

We are the Society for the Promotion of Good Grammar, but we've always secretly wished we were cool and beautiful enough to hang with the likes of you members of the Academy of Television Arts & Sciences. We've even tried taking our glasses off and releasing our hair from its usually severe bun to see if this makes us Hollywood-sexy. This always seems to work on TV. Without our glasses on, however, we are unable to evaluate the results, and we don't feel right asking our small children what they think.

But we digress. In truth, we're writing to pitch a few television shows. That is what you call it, isn't it? Pitching? Nice work! You've taken that term and made it your own! A slam dunk! No, wait—not that. We never mix our metaphors, and we consider the forthcoming ideas to be home runs, every last one of them.

We've noticed you often build an entire show around a cliché—and we mean that in the best possible sense of overused expression. For example:

Facts of Life: About girls from different sides of the track growing up under the watchful eye of an unmarried schoolmarm. Precious!

Diff'rent Strokes: African American brothers get to live in the penthouse suite of a rich white man and his freckle-nosed daughter. What could go wrong with those kids?

Family Ties: A middle-class white family with hippie parents tries to figure out how they ended up with a conservative Republican son who—in a stroke of master wit—wears neckties!

With this in mind, we've attached a list of television shows that we think are the bee's knees. (This, by the way, could be a really cute cartoon about an elderly bumblebee that needs a cane or two to get around. Baby boomers would eat it up with a spoon, or, if they're missing their teeth, suck it through a nourishment straw.)

The Nick of Time: A comedy about a time-traveling boy named Nick who turns back the clock to undo errors in his life, only to create new problems that must be solved in upcoming episodes. In the pilot, Nick tries to kiss Becky, only to get a slap in the face when he learns she already has a boyfriend. So he undoes his error, only to get a slap in the face when he tells Becky that yes, those pants do make her butt look big. Will he ever learn? Will the boy get the girl? Or will the slaps stick? Wait and see. . . .

Easy As Pi: The advanced math club at Miles High School is running perfectly well until Beatrice, a rebel with a clue—about polynomial equations, anyway—transfers from the inner-city school across town. Will she fit into this elite team of mathletes? Will she be the secret weapon the kids need to win the national competition in Washington, D.C.? Only if Beatrice learns to be a team player. And that, people, turns out to be as easy as pi. Which is to say, not easy in the slightest. Alternate title: *The Miles High Club*, which allows for the possibility of acute attraction between even the most obtuse teens.

Altared States: Michelle DuBois is a wedding planner with a heart of gold. But if she sees a mismatched couple about to tie the knot, she interferes until all is well in the world. And if she sees soul mates waiting in the wings, she does everything she can to ensure true love conquers all. It's no wonder she's the busiest wedding coordinator in Loveland, Colorado!

You Can Say That Again: Pete Repeat is the beloved parrot who *really* runs Noah's Ark, a pet store owned by the lonely, lovesick Noah Zarque. Time and time again, Noah pours out his heart to Pete, only to have Pete repeat his secrets at the most inopportune times. It's hilarious—and you can say that again!

We also have in development pitches for shows called:

Kat's Pajamas: a comedy about a copywriter who won't change out of her PJs until she sells a Hollywood screenplay;

That's the Ticket: a bittersweet comedy about a group of coworkers who won the lottery and can't decide how to divide the winnings;

The Bottom Line: a reality show based on a year in the life of a Weight Watchers support group; and

The Buck Stops Here: a drama about a man named Buck who travels across country after his wife has died, and finds love in the most unexpected place—a bed-and-breakfast run by a former nun. But will Buck stop? Or will this be one spot the Buck passes?

We will be sitting on pins and needles (a drama about three generations of women, war widows, all of them, who run a sewing and knitting shop in the Adirondacks) as we await your response.

Sincerely,

SPOGG

CLICHÉS: ALL IN DUE TIME

Even if you're not pitching a comedy, drama, or reality series to Hollywood, there are other times you can get away with using a cliché. Take weddings and funerals, for example. Here, familiar phrases—"dearly beloved," "the shadow of the valley of death"—can be the very things that offer credibility and comfort, as long as they're said by some religious official holding a leather-bound notebook. This constitutes the equivalent of the cliché hall pass.

Here are two more.

Cliché-Friendly Zone No. 1:
When You've Spawned

All prospective parents should be required to write down a list of things they will never say to their children because they are too idealistic for such mindless pap. Then they should put them into a sealed envelope, only to open them when they've finally given up hope. Each such statement is a useful alternative to boxing your children's ears once their newborn preciousness has been replaced with toddler puckishness. The following parental clichés, while overworked and factually suspect, are classics:

Because I said so, that's why. (Alternative: Because I'm the mother/father, that's why.)
If you keep making that face, it's going to freeze that way.
Go to your room and think about what you've done.
On the count of three . . .
Santa is watching.

Don't make me come up there.
I don't care who started it; I'm going to finish it.
Use your napkin, not your sleeve.
They're wherever you left them.
Wait till your (other parent) gets home.

Cliché-Friendly Zone No. 2: When You're Seeking a New Job

Career magazines wisely advise job candidates to leave the nose rings at home when they're looking for employment. This is because making individual statements frightens and repels The Man, who, for the most part, does all the hiring in this world. To impress The Man, the job seeker should use the following clichés, and in this order:

I'm a team player. (During the interview.)
I talk the talk and walk the walk.
Show me the money. (But only after receiving an offer.)
You get what you pay for. (When negotiating for more.)
Read the fine print. (Before accepting the offer.)

TOO MUCH OF A GOOD THING (SORRY)

If you're a vegetarian, skip ahead to SPOGG's grammar avenger character, who looks like this: . What follows will disgust you.

Stop reading now, Mr. and Ms. Won't Eat Anything with a Face. Really. We mean it.

There.

We can now talk meat without feeling guilty. Anyone who's ever cooked meat knows the fat is where the flavor is. Only suckers pay a premium for "extra-lean" ground beef. Those burgers end up tasting like sweaters. To a certain extent, the same is true in writing. It is possible to trim away all the fat, but with that can go a lot of personality. That's not always the case. Hemingway was able to write satisfying, lean prose. But he didn't exactly die in bed as a contented old man, now, did he? Perhaps developing a tolerance for the occasional adjective or weary phrase might have done the man some good.

Hemingway aside, there's definitely such a thing as too much fat. Lest your readers spit out your words in their napkins, here are some obese phrases you can almost always stand to shed, along with succinct alternatives. There are more out there, but hey—you get what you pay for.

Flabby Clichés to Trim

between a rock and a hard place: He has a difficult choice. He's in a tough spot. Neither option looks good.

born with a silver spoon in his mouth: Privileged. Spoiled. Although we take metal spoons for granted these days, they used to be made from "spons," or chips of wood. Wealthy godparents would give silver spoons as baptism gifts. The cliché can be turned sideways for comic effect, as former Texas governor Ann Richards did in 1988 when she said George Bush was born with a silver foot in his mouth.

buckle down to work: Get serious. Start working.

bury the hatchet: Make peace. Forgive. Stop fighting.

by hook or by crook: Somehow. By any means possible.

by the skin of one's teeth: Barely.

dead as a doornail: Dead.

dumb as a dodo: It's smarter just to use "dumb" (though it's certainly not nice).

even steven: Even, fair, or equitable.

from the word go: From the start. Immediately.

fumble the play: Fumble.

get a rise out of someone: Antagonize, irritate, vex.

get (or keep) the ball rolling: Start, initiate, sustain, perpetuate, or persevere. Political campaigns weren't always as nasty, brutish, and long as they are now. What's more, they had better props. William Henry Harrison's presidential campaign supporters rolled ten-foot-high victory balls made of tin and leather for journeys of up to three hundred miles, asking voters to "keep the ball rolling for the log cabin and hard-cider candidate." The phrase originated earlier with a game called bandy, which is similar to hockey and totally boring if the ball isn't moving.

gird your loins: Protect, ready, prepare. Not that you were thinking this, but this expression has practical origins that have nothing to do with contraception. In the Bible, when the prophet Elijah girds his loins, he's merely tucking in his robe.

give someone a leg up: Help, advantage.

give the slip: Escape, ditch.

gone to Davy Jones's locker: Dead.

go to bat for: Defend, advocate.

have a chip on your shoulder: Easily offended. Looking for a fight. Feeling inferior. Newspaper accounts from the 1800s describe boys literally placing chunks of wood on their shoulders, daring people to knock them off. The actor Robert Conrad gave the cliché a 1970s twist by daring TV viewers to dislodge an Eveready battery, much to the amusement of Johnny Carson. What's next, an iPod? Oh, we dare you. . . .

have a full plate: Busy.

honest to goodness: Pure flab. Eliminate altogether.

in the family way: Pregnant.

in the nick of time: In time.

keep a stiff upper lip: Remain stoic. Conceal emotion. Don't cry.

kick the bucket: Die.

knight in shining armor: Savior. Hero.

leave no stone unturned: Be thorough.

left in the lurch: Left behind. Abandoned.

let the cat out of the bag: Reveal.

like a kid in a candy shop: Happy. Excited. Delirious. Chuffed. Thrilled.

lion's share: The most. Unfair portion. Biggest piece.

make a mountain out of a molehill: Exaggerate. Inflate.

march to a different drummer: Independent. Unique. Quirky.

meanwhile, back at the ranch: Meanwhile.

mend fences: Forgive. Make peace.

mile a minute: Quickly.

mop / wipe the floor with: Defeat. Rout. Clobber.

more fun than a barrel of monkeys: Really fun.

nest egg: Savings.

on the fence: Undecided. Waffling. Vacillating.

open sesame: Open.

out of the running: Eliminated. Defeated.

pay through the nose: Overpay.

pick someone's brain: Discuss. Question.

put the kibosh on it: Stop. Prevent.

quiet as a lamb / mouse: Quiet. Silent. Hushed.

raining cats and dogs: Raining. Pouring. (Old man is snoring.)

right off the bat: Initially. Immediately. From the start.

right under your nose: Obvious. Apparent. Plainly visible.

shoot one's mouth off: Yammer. Blather. Gush. Spew.

shout from the rooftops: Broadcast. Blare. Holler. Shout.

sit up and take notice: Notice. Observe. Perceive.

sorry state of affairs: Pathetic.

spick-and-span: Clean.

spill the beans: Reveal.

stab in the back: Betray.

start from scratch: Start over. Begin again.

take a hike: Leave. Scram. Depart.

the coast is clear: We're safe. No one's watching.

throw off the scent: Distract.

throw your hat in the ring: Attempt. Try. Enter.

walk on eggshells: To be wary. To be cautious. To be tactful.

wash one's hands of: To quit. To dismiss. To disregard.

waving a red flag: To antagonize. To provoke.

weathered the storm: Survived.

yes, no, maybe so: I don't know.

you can bet your bottom dollar: You bet. Yes. Certainly.

you could have heard a pin drop: It was quiet. No one spoke.

9

The Enemy Within—Flab, Jargon, and the People in Your Office

**The Society for the Promotion
of Good Grammar**

MEMORANDUM

TO:REPRESENTATIVE BENNIE G. THOMPSON, CHAIRMAN

OF THE HOUSE OF REPRESENTATIVES HOMELAND

SECURITY COMMITTEE

FROM:THE SOCIETY FOR THE PROMOTION OF GOOD

GRAMMAR

SUBJECT:JARGON: THREAT LEVEL

ORANGE

We are the Society for the Promotion of Good Grammar, and we're writing to report a severe jargon hazard at the Department of Homeland Security. To use the department's own color-coding system, the gobbledygook on the Web site is at a level orange.

We urge you to remind the DHS of two things:

1. Officials should use the full range of colors available. Otherwise, they dilute the meaning of the ones they actually use. The first fourteen times they changed the threat level, they simply toggled between yellow and orange. It wasn't until five years after the 9/11 attacks that we saw our first red. Why even bother having blue and green if they're never used?

The department's own Web site says "there continues to be no credible, specific intelligence to suggest an imminent threat to the homeland at this time." If that's the case, then we should be living with a blue rating for "general risk of terrorist attack."

If the words and colors don't line up, we'll stop looking to the government as a meaningful source of information. This is terrible for democracy.

2. The way they explain color changes breaks several rules of plain language. According to the Center for Plain Language, government agencies should:

- write reasonably short sentences;
- favor the active voice;
- use clear, informative headings;
- use logical organization; and
- omit unnecessary words

We'll quote from the Homeland Security Department's Web site:

Color-coded Threat Level System is used to communicate with public safety officials and the public at-large [*sic*] through a threat-based, color-coded system so that protective measures can be implemented to reduce the likelihood or impact of an attack. Raising the threat condition has economic, physical, and psychological effects on the nation; [*sic*] so, the Homeland Security Advisory System can place specific geographic regions or industry sectors on a higher alert status than other regions or industries, based on specific threat information.

Here's how the department could have written this:

We use colors to alert you to possible terrorist activity, so everyone can do what's necessary to prevent attacks and reduce their effects. Raising the threat level can be expensive, inconvenient, and stressful. We sometimes limit our alerts to certain places or industries, if we have information that warrants it.

Sincerely,
SPOGG

Plain language is a civil right.

—FORMER VICE PRESIDENT AL GORE

Some of us who are passionate about grammar get sheepish about our zeal. *Oh, don't mind me. I'm just a funny old lady with plastic fruit on my hat. It's not as though good grammar is a matter of life and death. Who wants some nice rib-bon candy?*

We need to knock that off, all of it—the sheepishness, the plastic fruit, and the idea that clean, grammatical language is merely a hobby. Collecting bottle caps is a hobby. Building boats out of milk cartons is a hobby. Cockfighting, ventriloquism: these are hobbies—even if one is illegal and the other should be.

Mastering the English language serves a higher purpose, and perhaps even a heroic one. Anyone who tells you otherwise hasn't heard the story of Chrissie Maher, a gray-haired, teapot-shaped British matriarch who's dedicated her life to what she calls Plain English. Her crusade started about thirty years ago, during winter in northern England. Ms. Maher was trying to help two old ladies fill out a government form that would have given them money to heat their home, but the form bewildered her. She promised the women she'd return the next day, which she did, only to watch them speed off in an ambulance. Both elderly women were dead within a week from the effects of hypothermia.

It wasn't that they were stupid or uneducated. They'd been teachers. Rather, the form was so badly written and so full of jargon, they couldn't figure out how to fill it out properly. It killed them, and in the sad aftermath, Ms. Maher launched the Plain English Campaign. The group's mission is to combat "jargon, gobbledygook, and other confusing language while promoting crystal-clear language." Its members want the documents we use to make decisions—forms, contracts, brochures, and the like—to be written so we can understand them and act on them the first time we read them.

It's the only way democracy can thrive, Ms. Maher argues.

Of course, there are people who are not moved by either democracy or the clattering of elderly bones. It's all about the
money. The bottom line for such people is that plain English
saves money. There are some excellent statistics on this, also
from England. The British government reviewed its forms in
the early 1980s and ended up saving about $18 million in print-
ing and storage costs by the time it was done. It's even more
expensive when people fill out forms incorrectly. A study on
the Department of Health and Social Security estimated that
errors on the old forms cost England about $1.3 billion a year.

The United States has its plain-language advocates, as well.
A group of federal employees has formed PLAIN, the Plain
Language Action and Information Network. Their mission is
to translate government gobbledygook, a word coined in 1944
by the *New York Times Magazine* writer Maury Maverick to mean
"long, pompus, vague [writing], usually with Latinized words."
There's also an international organization called PLAIN, which
stands for Plain Language Association International. This
group supports and promotes people who work as writers, editors, and in other jobs where clear English is paramount.

Say what you will about President Nixon, the man was an
early friend to plain language, as well as respectable (and
plain) Republican cloth coats. In 1972, he demanded that the
journal of emerging government regulations called the
Federal Register be written in everyday language. President
Carter wrote an executive order designed to make regulations
clearer and more cost effective. Then President Reagan undid
that work, an interesting move for a man known as the Great
Communicator. At least in his death there is some truth in advertising; the spot at the Reagan Library where journalists

were sequestered during the first debate in 2007 by Republican presidential candidates was called "the Spin Room."

Given the irony of the Great Communicator designation, it's probably no surprise that the president dubbed "Slick Willie" was the next to take up the plain-English cause. President Clinton wrote this memo January 1, 1999, directing it mainly at his fellow lawyers:

> By using plain language, we send a clear message about what the government is doing, what it requires, and what services it offers. . . . Plain language documents have logical organization; common, everyday words, except for necessary technical terms; "you" and other pronouns; the active voice; and short sentences.

Clinton gave us a good example of plain (if not entirely accurate language) when he said, "I did not have sex with that woman, Miss Lewinsky." He also found time to assign Vice President Gore to monitor plain language in government. Gore took to handing out "No Gobbledygook" awards for well-edited government communication. One went to the author of those stickers you see on SUVs warning drivers they're more likely to tip. Here's the old warning note:

> This is a multipurpose passenger vehicle which will handle and maneuver differently from an ordinary passenger car, in driving conditions which may occur on streets and highways and off road. As with other vehicles of this type, if you make sharp turns or abrupt maneuvers, the vehicle may roll over or may go out of control and crash. You

should read driving guidelines and instructions in the Owner's Manual, and WEAR YOUR SEAT BELTS AT ALL TIMES.

After revision, the sticker showed a picture of a tipping car, a seat-belted driver, and the following text:

WARNING: HIGHER ROLLOVER RISK. Avoid abrupt maneuvers and excessive speed. Always buckle up. See owner's manual for further information.

It's not perfect, but it's certainly better. (We would have written "Don't swerve or speed" instead of "avoid abrupt maneuvers and excessive speed.")

THE ENEMIES OF PLAIN LANGUAGE

Generally, two things separate plain language from its convoluted counterpart: extra words and jargon. Letting sentences and paragraphs run on complicates things, too. Those problems can be fixed with punctuation—especially the period—and the Enter key. So we will focus on wordiness for now, and move later to jargon.

Believe it or not, a government agency has some pretty good advice on this score. In its writing guide, the Federal Aviation Administration includes a useful table that shows the difference between plain and bloated prose. If you find yourself using any of the expressions on the left, stop it. Replace them with the shorter, clearer choices on the right, and your readers will thank you.

EXCESS WORDS	PLAIN LANGUAGE
accordingly	so
addressees	you
as a means of	to
as prescribed by	in, under
at a later date	later
at the present time	now
commence	begin, start

ELEVEN OTHER WAYS WE BLOAT SENTENCES

With both cat skinning and sentence padding, there are multiple methods, and unfortunately, no clear rules on how much is too much. (Though with cat skinning, we'd argue that any amount is excessive.) Some successful writers make their reputations by sticking mostly with nouns and verbs. Others can't resist the siren call of adverbs and other voluptuous modifiers. The epitaph of J. K. Rowling could easily read, "She truly, madly, deeply loved adverbs." She's the richest author in the world, so you can't say the most successful sentences are the most spare.

Even readability tests, which use eye-goggling mathematical formulas based on syllable counts and sentence lengths to measure the readability of your prose, have their limits. The Gunning Fog Index, for example, rates the first few pages of James Joyce's *Finnegans [sic] Wake* at a 6.64—easier than *Reader's Digest*, but a bit more challenging than *TV Guide*. The three main readability tests rate the entire book as an easier read than most. Some graduate students in English might disagree (or feel an urge to put rocks in their pockets and stroll into the ocean). Here's that first sentence, so you can judge for yourself (we're holding out for the *Reader's Digest* version):

> *riverrun, past Eve and Adam's, from swerve of shore to bend of bay, brings us by a commodius vicus of recirculation back to Howth Castle and Environs.*

Whatever your writing style, there are some words that usually fail to punch up your prose. Try using the "find and replace" function in your word processor to skim these dozen flabby words and phrases from your sentences:

1. To be, or be plus -ing: An easy way to lose weight in your writing.
I should be sleeping.
I should sleep.
I need to be sleeping.
I need to sleep.

2. Began/started: A clue you're clearing your throat instead of starting to make your point.
He began to understand she wasn't human, after all.
He understood she wasn't human, after all.

3. Could/would: Can often be cut.
He would swim daily in the pond.
He swam daily in the pond.
She could see his Speedo.
She saw his Speedo.

4. Just, essentially, actually, basically, really, totally, quite, very, extremely, moreover, as it were, it can be seen that/should be noted that: Often these word are ~~just~~ filler. ~~It should be noted that~~ the same goes for rather and quite. They're ~~quite~~ unnecessary.

5. Overdescribing: "Grave danger"—is there any other kind? Likewise, "exact copy" and "free gift" are redundant.

6. Passive constructions: In these, the sentence subject has the action performed on it, instead of performing the action.
The book was written by J. K. Rowling.
J. K. Rowling wrote the book.

7. Up, down, out, and back: If direction is implied, don't use it.
He sat ~~down~~.
She spread the newspaper ~~out~~ on the table.
She stood ~~up~~.
He looked ~~back~~ at the wreckage of the canoe.

8. That: used more than is necessary. He knew ~~that~~ the dog was neutered.

9. There are/these are/this is the: Very often, these ~~are the~~ signal ~~of~~ flabby formations.

10. To the: Little words that add little meaning.
I have lost many pieces to the puzzle.
I have lost many puzzle pieces.

11. Was: Linking verbs like this can often be compressed.

She was singing.

She sang.

BUZZWORDS: ANOTHER GREAT EVIL

Wordiness is bad. It slows comprehension and causes boredom. Jargon—particularly the kind known as buzzwords—is worse. There are a few loopholes. Doctors, lawyers, and other professionals use jargon that's specific to their professions. We're perfectly happy for surgeons, for example, to name their various knives and needles specific things, instead of saying, "Nurse, hand me the pointy thing over there. The one that isn't bloody yet."

Buzzwords, by contrast, have no merit. Buzzwords are the fungus of language. They spread so that even the most vigilant person finds herself discussing, 24/7, which of her action items could be classified as low-hanging fruit. These phrases coat our hands with slime, making it difficult to pick up the straightforward substitutes.

In our Workplace Buzzwords Hall of Lame, we call out ten categories of phrases that need to go.

1. **Dentist envy:** Most office workers wouldn't know a drill from a driver, but you wouldn't know it from all the talk of **drilling down** that goes on in the office. Is "studying the details" too boring? Are we hoping to tap into an oil well and, like Jed Clampett, move to Beverly ("Hills, that is")?

2. **Nature's calling:** Is that **blue-sky thinking**? Or perhaps a **green-grass** (or **green-field**) **scenario**? We

prefer the more mundane "creative thinking," or even the tired-out "brainstorming." At least that's just one word.

3. **The computer virus:** It's bad enough when people clack away on their laptops during meetings, and use instant-messaging software to chat with people who are sitting five feet away. It's worse, though, when they use computer jargon to talk with each other. **Let's take this offline.** It's not a **binary issue**, and we don't have **the bandwidth** to resolve it now. Translation: "We can talk about this after the meeting. There's no yes-or-no answer, and we don't have enough time to work it out right now."

4. **Insincerity reigns.** Anyone who says **with all due respect** is saying "I have no respect for you." And when people say, **Let me play devil's advocate**, it really means, "Your idea is Satanic, and here's why." What's wrong with a straightforward "I disagree"?

5. **I change clothes in a phone booth:** Some jargon is for people with a secret superhero complex. These **change agents** call their task lists **action items**. Although they can't leap tall buildings in a single bound they can turn the four-letter word **work** into the twelve-letter **deliverables**.

6. **Ain't nothin' but a noun dog:** Many nouns do double duty as verbs, but when there is a perfectly lovely verb to use, why bastardize a noun? (Unless you get to say "bastardize"; that one gets a free pass.) "Dialogue" is a noun. "Talk" and "discuss" are two verbs that work far better than **dialogue** as a verb. Here's an unintentionally

ironic example of excessive noun-dogging from a company that wants to help people get better results when they dial customer-support services: "Organizations should use this data to **trend** improvement over time, to **bonus** call center executives, to **impact** support representatives' compensation and training, and to **benchmark** against the industry."

7. **Bloatmeal:** The American workweek gets longer every year, and the habit of using several words where one will do is partly to blame. "Now" means the same thing as **at this juncture** or **at this point in time**. Same with **at the present. At the end of the day,** which usually can be eliminated (along with the cliché that's likely to follow), means the same thing as "ultimately," saving five words until they're actually needed.

8. **Foul ball:** Sports metaphors stink. Do not **step up to the plate.** Do not **hit the ground running.** Don't even think of **running with the ball.** You will not **hit it out of the park** if you talk this way.

9. **Porky, meet Hammy:** In addition to being wordy, some annoying office-isms are also cheesy. They're the big plaid golf pants of the office lexicon. No one should have to look at them, or hear people discuss assumptions that are **baked in,** proposals that are **buttoned up,** or descriptions of people getting either **their ducks in a row** or **down to brass tacks. Give me a jingle** sounds like a human resources violation. And if anyone says **open the kimono** when he means **show how it works,** feel free to file a textual harassment suit.

10. **I didn't need to see that:** Speaking of **opening the kimono,** there are certain expressions that evoke horrors. For people with imagination, certain phrases can cause trauma. **Touch base** and **close the loop** are mildly icky. The **blow-by-blow** is worse. And the expression **low-hanging fruit** calls to mind certain body parts that succumb to gravity's grip as we age. Please, stop with the plucking. Isn't it easier just to say easy?

This Is Your Business on Flab

∗

We found this passage online at a company called BusinessTown [sic]. We've capitalized all the unforgivable jargon, wordiness, and clichés, which didn't leave much ~~marketing copy.~~ Would you trust this company's business advice?

Study, Block and Tackle!

Study, but don't necessarily copy [sic] *your competitor's moves. Visit their businesses, watch their ads, figure out their strategies, and find their ACHILLES* [sic] *HEELS! Always WATCH THEM LIKE A HAWK!*

You may not be able to keep up with your competitor's [sic] *strategy* [sic] *MOVE BY MOVE. You should, however, be READY AND ABLE to blunt or block the IMPACT of their moves. Then, later, you can make your own OFFENSIVE*

*MOVE AT YOUR OWN PACE and in your OWN BALL COURT.
[As opposed to those shuttlecock courts all the cool kids
have?]*

*For example, let's say you are selling a product on a
NATIONAL BASIS through RETAIL OUTLETS. You discover
that your competitor is about TO LAUNCH a gigantic, [sic]
multimillion dollar [sic] advertising campaign. [It's never
a small multimillion-dollar campaign, is it?] You don't
have the time or money to create a competing campaign.
What you may be able to do, though, is offer a SPECIAL
ONE-TIME DEAL TO THE TRADE—something like buy five
items, get one free—for a LIMITED PERIOD OF TIME. This
way, you can STOCK UP THE TRADE and limit the SHELF
SPACE that is available to your competition. The added
CONSUMER TRAFFIC attributable to your competitor's
ADVERTISING EFFORTS will LARGELY benefit your prod-
uct since it is the AVAILABLE PRODUCT. AT A LATER
POINT IN TIME you can LAUNCH your own MARKETING
EFFORT or PRODUCT INTRODUCTION—perhaps during a
typically slow period for your competitor.*

The great enemy of clear language is insincerity.

—GEORGE ORWELL

JARGON: THE WORST LANGUAGE
SIN OF ALL

Worse than buzzwords, though, is language meant to fudge reality. The author and linguist William Lutz calls this third category "doublespeak," and it's what happens when people either want to obscure the truth, or don't think critically about the words they're choosing, and instead, mindlessly repeat mushy phrases. Why else did our government try to pass off a proposal that weakened the Clean Air Act as the "Clear Skies" initiative? It's why corporations no longer fire people, or even lay them off; they "downsize." It's how destructive bombing campaigns are passed off as "surgical strikes" that sometimes result in "collateral damage," instead of assaults that kill unarmed men, women, children, and old people.

It's how the body bags of the Vietnam era have come to be called "transfer tubes." And it's why, when politicians lie, newspaper reporters are more likely to call it a "fictionalization" or a "misstatement." There's no commandment against fiction, so why should any of us feel outraged or abused when this happens?

The National Council of Teachers of English gives awards for doublespeak, dubious honors that call out some of the most misleading speech of the year. It's courageous for these teachers, who don't shrink from tackling even the most powerful people in the nation. President George W. Bush has won at least twice, most recently for "the inspired invention of the phrase 'weapons of mass destruction–related program activities' "—whatever that means. He also won for saying, "These are open forums; you're able to come and listen to what I have to say." His former defense secretary Donald Rumsfeld, meanwhile, was acknowledged for calling the Abu Ghraib torture "the excesses of human nature that humanity suffers."

Humanity suffers, all right.

But we don't have to put up with bloated, misleading communication. Like the national teachers' organization, we can pounce on bad language where we find it, and demand something better. We can, and we must.

A TALE FROM THE TRENCHES

Ken Barnes, who writes about music for *USA Today*, worked at Microsoft when the company first developed content for movie and music buffs. Barnes took a word lover's delight in the sometimes perverse jargon that pelted his ears. As a joke, he and some like-minded colleagues started a lexicon of Microspeak, which included several dozen oddball words that flew around the company's offices, including:

bucket: a category or virtual container;
slipping: missing a deadline; and
disintermediate: to eliminate the middle man.

Sadly, the joke turned out to be on Barnes and his friends. Microsoft's earnest company newsletter featured a front-page story on the effort. Instead of picking up on Barnes's embarrassment, the newsletter called the company jargon "pretty cool" and "not unlike English itself." Then the editors published their own version of Microspeak, so that the dreaded jargon could not only survive, but flourish.

We never said this would be easy.

10.

Rules That Never Were, Are No More, and Should Be Broken

The Society for the Promotion of Good Grammar

Dear Crabby Grammar Person:

We are writing because you apparently missed the memo. The following so-called grammatical errors aren't actually errors:

1. It's not always wrong to split an infinitive, and sometimes, it's even a better choice.

2. You can start a sentence with a conjunction.

3. Sentence fragments aren't necessarily evil.

4. You can end a sentence with a preposition.

Please stop with the outraged letters to the editor, the stern looks, and the meaningful sighs. And buck up, glowering camper: it's still barbaric to say "irregard-less."

    Sincerely,

    SPOGG

    Some beliefs are harder to surrender than others. When we first noticed that Santa Claus and our mother had the same handwriting, we realized—with a pang—that they were the same person. It took us longer to figure out that the place our parents called "Country Sunshine" was really just the anonymous concrete turn-around at the end of our dead-end street. All those trips they encouraged us to take there had one purpose, and it was not to warm our skin in the miraculous rain-free air. They just wanted us out of the house. We were in our midtwenties when we figured this out. How humiliating.

    Likewise, it can be a tough thing to learn that Sister Sheila had it all wrong when she said, "Thou shalt not end a sentence with a preposition" and "Thou shalt not start a sentence with a conjunction." We trusted her, with her no-nonsense lips and liver-spotted hands. In defense of the well-intentioned nuns and grammar teachers, they were not like our fabulist parents, making intentional misstatements. The nuns did not mean to lead us astray. They no doubt had trusted elders of their own, urging starchy and relentlessly proper prose at every turn. In short, their elders gave the nuns bad habits.

    And so it is that those of us who care about language have found ourselves staring at a pile of mythical grammar rules that have no more truth or depth than a desert mirage, because they didn't spring from the organic soil of emerging English, but were added later for one reason or another (that reason usually being outsized love of Latin). With enduring gratitude to the nuns and English teachers of our past, we urge you to leave Country Sunshine behind you. It was a cul-de-sac, after all. How good can a place like that really be?

THE TEN FALSE COMMANDMENTS OF THE ENGLISH LANGUAGE

False Commandment Number One: Thou Shalt Not End a Sentence with a Preposition

There's a famous, if spurious, Winston Churchill quote rejecting this rule as "something up with which I will not put." Even if he never said this, the point is good. We don't need a rule that often requires us to complicate our syntax. Compare these sentences:

Where does he come from?

From where does he come?

The first is easier to understand because the important information comes at the beginning of the sentence.

Language historians say we laid claim to this Country Sunshine acreage in part because of our tendency to idealize Latin. In Latin, the prefix *pre* means "before." A "pre-position" couldn't be positioned last, could it? Well, yes it could. Even Shakespeare did it.

There are certain times, though, when it's ugly. "Where's he at?" is one of those times. "Where is he?" is better form. The "at" is unnecessary, and you'll never go wrong striking such words . . . out.

False Commandment Number Two: Thou Shalt Not Split Your Infinitives

The Roman Empire is long gone, but its influence remains. There are good reasons. As they say in *Monty Python's Life of Brian*, "All right, but apart from the sanitation, medicine, education, wine, public order, irrigation, roads, the fresh water system and public health, what have the Romans ever done for us?"

It's no wonder certain old-timey grammarians, in love with the wonders of Latin, wanted to spread some of its luster on English. The ban on splitting infinitives is a case in point. In Latin, an infinitive is one word. It can't be split any more than you can split ye s and n o. In English, though, an infinitive is to + a verb (to run, for example). You're not supposed to insert any words between to and run.

In most cases, it's just as well to follow this so-called rule, especially because there are persnickety people out there who are not yet ready to learn that Santa, Country Sunshine, and the solemn words of Sister Sheila are not literal truths. The point of writing and speaking is to be understood, and if people get hung up on your allegedly bad grammar, you'll fail in that critical mission.

But sometimes, following rules just to please the well-meaning purists is a bad idea. The famous line from *Star Trek* is a good example: "To boldly go where no man has gone before" would have lost much of its poetry if Gene Roddenberry had been a prig and written "To go, boldly, where no man has gone before." It's not just iambic pentameter that's sacrificed when we give in to senseless word-order hang-ups; it's clarity. If the president is planning *to almost triple* your taxes to pay for a Humvee for every garage (chickens in pots are so Depression-era), then splitting the infinitive helps get that meaning across. It's much better than saying, *the president plans almost to triple your taxes,* because that makes it sound like the Humvee plan is half-baked. And to *triple almost your taxes* doesn't make any sense at all, unless you're trying to capture the dialect of a talking robot with a bad battery pack.

False Commandment Number Three: Use "That" with Restrictive Clauses, "Which" with Nonrestrictive Clauses

This rule happens to be one we like. Here's how it's supposed to work:

When you have a clause that adds necessary information to the sentence, you use "that." When you have a clause that adds expendable information, you use "which," and set it off with a comma.

I brushed the dog that barked.

I brushed the dog, which barked.

These two sentences are darned similar. The first, though, shows that you brushed the barking dog. The second indicates that the dog barked because of your brushing. That little pause added by the comma gives the dog time to yap in protest to the grooming session.

Now, had you written, "I brushed the dog which barked," the meaning would be the same as the first. Enough skilled writers used "which" this way to make it legitimate. (Even E. B. White did it, after expressly advising other writers not to.) It sounds a tad more pompous than "that," and sharp-penciled editors would probably change the word, but it's not an error.

But you can't use "that" for clauses that are set off by commas. It just wouldn't do to write, "I brushed the dog, that barked"; this looks like a comma splice. So this is perhaps where the stricture against using "which" in restrictive clauses emerged. "Which" can stand in for "that," but the reverse is not the case.

False Commandment Number Four: It's Wrong to Start a Sentence with "and" or "but"

Writers have been doing this for more than a thousand years, so you'd think the people who insist that it's wrong would give up. But they don't.

The coordinating conjunctions—"and," "but," "for," "yet," "nor," "or," and "so"—link ideas together. They can link ideas within a sentence, or they can link the ideas expressed between two closely related sentences. It can make your writing choppy if you do this too much, but it's an effective way to emphasize contrasts and connections.

False Commandment Number Five: "None" Comes from "Not One" or "No One," and Is Therefore Always Singular

It's comforting to hear when things are "always" one way or the other. Life and language are (almost) always more complicated. From the seventeenth to the nineteenth centuries, for example, "none" was usually considered plural. Today, it goes both ways:

None of the movies were worth watching.

None of the movie was worth watching.

The trick is, if you can swap out "not any of them" for "none," then your sentence needs a plural verb. If you can swap out "not any of it," go with the singular.

Not any of them were worth watching.

Not any of it was worth watching.

False Commandment Number Six: "Since" Must Always Refer to Time

The *Oxford English Dictionary*, which tracks the usage of words in print, shows people have been using "since" in reference to time since around the year 1450. Long time, no? It's therefore understandable that some people insist "since" cannot also be used to mean "because." There is just one problem with that. The *OED* also traces the first use of "since" as a synonym for "because" to . . . the very same decade. This isn't one of those words that started one way and veered in another direction; our most reliable sources tell us it's always run both ways.

It is true that the words aren't interchangeable. You can't say, "I've been awake because five o'clock this morning" (unless you named your child or cat "five o'clock this morning," in which case, you deserve all that happens to you).

False Commandment Number Seven: Don't Use "Like" as a Conjunction

If you're writing for a formal outlet—let's say *Tuxedo Times*—then by all means, use "as" instead of "like" as a conjunction. "I look swell, as anyone would when dressed in fine evening wear."

But if you are speaking or writing informally, it's fine to use "like" as a conjunction. "I look great, like I should in my tight tuxedo T-shirt!"

"Like" used as a conjunction earned infamy in 1954, when it was used as part of a tobacco company's slogan: "Winston tastes good like a cigarette should." Apparently Walter Cronkite refused to read it in his broadcast (he objected to the grammar, not to the carcinogenic nature of the product). In truth, "like" has a long history of appearing as a conjunction. Chaucer used it this way, as did Marlowe and Shakespeare.

Even so, many people bristle at this usage. This is one of those nonrules worth obeying, just so people don't think you're a rube. It's sort of like soup slurping. Though it's considered rude here, it's polite—even complimentary—elsewhere. It doesn't change the soup a bit, just the reputation of the person with the spoon. So if you want to be respected *and* understood, don't use "like" as a conjunction in educated or persnickety company. If you want to have fun, then feel free to pop in Prince's "Party Like It's 1999" song without a twinge of guilt. (At least not because of the grammar.)

False Commandment Number Eight: You Must Say "It Is I" If You Wish to Be Correct

There are a number of boring and technical reasons "This is I" and "This is she" are grammatically correct. Summarized for sanity's sake, the verb "to be" can't take an object. So, when it's used, the subject and the pronoun that follows must be in the same case, or so say the strict grammarians. It is he; it is I; we are they . . . the list goes on. There's just one problem with this. Two, actually. The first is that the logic is based once again on the idea that English should ape Latin, which has no "it is me" construction. The second is one lawyers might use: precedent. Some four hundred years before Shakespeare had Ophelia say "Woe is me," English speakers were using "me" instead of "I." Long-term usage doesn't necessarily make it correct, but when you have otherwise rigid stylists such as E. B. White saying, "One is good grammar and the other is good sense," then it's reasonable to let this one go.

Where you do want to be careful, though, is with sentences like this: "He likes chocolate more than me," because the meaning is unclear. Do you mean he likes chocolate more than you do? Or he likes chocolate more than he likes you? If he likes chocolate more than you do, then you're better off saying, "He likes chocolate more than I do." If you're second in his heart, well, here: Have some chocolate. It'll make you feel better.

False Commandment Number Nine: You Must Always Use "Whom" When It's the Object of a Sentence

It's been more than two hundred years since Noah Webster first started writing about American English. Even he eventually agreed that a statement such as "Who is it for?" is more natural than "For whom is it?" So you have it on solid authority that it's okay to say "who" for "whom," especially in speech or informal writing contexts. Sometimes, "whom" is just a bit too stuffy.

This doesn't mean it's not important to know the rule, though. Use "who" as the subject of the sentence, and "whom" as an object. A subject performs the action; the object has the action performed on it.

False Commandment Number Ten:
Sentence Fragments Are Evil

Sometimes, sentence fragments are bad news. To be considered complete, sentences need subjects and predicates, even if the subject is sometimes just an understood one. You could make a great case that fragmented sentences are never grammatically correct, but there's a problem with this. A big one, especially when you consider language as an art form instead of a technical tool. Pick up any modern novel, and you are sure to find fragments. Perhaps even many of them. That's because, when used with purpose, fragments can add emphasis, rhythm, verisimilitude, and even clarity to prose. They probably don't belong in company memos, but anywhere you want to inject a more personal tone into your writing, they're fair game.

Mumpsimus or Sumpsimus?

If you're having a hard time letting go of these false grammar rules, you're not alone. Consider the case of the medieval monk who said *"quod in ore mumpsimus"* instead of *"quod in ore sumpsimus"* during the eucharist at his Latin mass. Most likely, the monk either couldn't read, or was using an incorrectly transcribed text. Either way, he couldn't part with his error. After forty years, he'd grown used to it, and said, "I will not change my old mumpsimus for your new sumpsimus."

Today, the word "mumpsimus" refers to someone stuck in his ways, evidence be damned.

LOST CAUSES: ERRORS WE CAN IGNORE

Bryan A. Garner, in his *Dictionary of Modern American Usage*, talks about words that have been "skunked," meaning they've turned putrid because of disputes over their acceptable uses. Some people stick with the traditional; others open their vocabulary to the new. There's no pleasing both groups. Savvy writers avoid the skunks, so that no readers are distracted by the smell. We can imagine ourselves here to be like wise and courageous generals who, despite their clanking collection of victory medals, sometimes look at their fellow warriors and say, "Let's pack it in, boys. This is one we're not going to win."

This sort of thing does happen with language, you know: we fight the good fight and lose, anyway. The lost causes:

We Can No Longer Take "Literally" Quite So Literally

It once meant actually true. Now, though, it's used *literally all the time* as an intensifier.

"Hopefully" No Longer Merely Means "in a Hopeful Manner"

Though many writers, current and former nuns, and teachers of English seize up in the bowels when it stands in as a shorter substitute for "it is hoped," it's still a common usage. Crusaders will have better luck taking their red pens elsewhere. And really, do we want people to start saying, "It is hoped that the weather will be balmy tomorrow"? Hopefully not.

We Cannot Require Our Children to Say "Shall" Instead of "Will" for Simple Future Tense

Grammar books used to insist the first-person future for both I and we was "shall." *I shall see you tomorrow, Lady Hedgerow!*

With I and we, the verb "will" had a specific function: to express intention, command, or desire. *I will defeat the Kaiser! I WILL!*

With sentences in the second and third person, however, these shall / will roles were reversed. *You shall bring his head to me!* Or, *He will see the doctor tomorrow about that rash.*

This distinction is pretty much dead, except when singing the protest song "We Shall Overcome." Grammatically speaking, that's ironic, for we shall not overcome the will of the masses on this issue.

"A Couple Of" Doesn't Always Require the "Of"

Though some find the expression "I read a couple books this summer" to be abominable without the "of," it's increasingly acceptable in informal contexts to drop that preposition. And indeed, there are some uses where the "of" is a bit precious. Imagine the person at the picnic stating his intention to eat a "couple of more" chips (or even the scholar saying, "I plan to read a couple of more books"). "A couple of" is already inexact, at least in its idiomatic sense; when paired with an also inexact word like "more," insisting on that "of" is a bit like cleaning a muddy pig with a greasy rag: hopeless.

No One Can Be Sent to Grammar Detention for Describing Food as "Healthy"

It is true that "healthful" means wholesome. But "healthy" has been used to mean the same thing since 1552, so those of us who experience unhealthful bouts of high blood pressure when we see an advertisement for "healthy cereal" need to find a new outlet for our consternation. Or, if we have a healthy appetites, we can always eat a few cookies.

ARE YOU READY TO BREAK THE RULES? HOW TO TELL

The movie *Finding Forrester* is worth seeing for anyone who loves language and writing. It's about a talented inner-city student who tracks down a reclusive writer and former teacher, William Forrester, played by the great Sean Connery. In this scene, Forrester critiques the writing of his student, Jamal:

> FORRESTER: *Paragraph three starts with a conjunction, "and." You should never start a sentence with a conjunction.*
> JAMAL: *Sure you can.*
> FORRESTER: *No. It's a firm rule.*
> JAMAL: *No. It was a firm rule. Sometimes using a conjunction at the start of a sentence . . . makes it stand out. And that may be what the writer's trying to do.*
> FORRESTER: *And what is the risk?*
> JAMAL: *Doing it too much. It's a distraction and could give your piece a run-on feeling. But the rule on using "and" or*

"but" at the start of a sentence is pretty shaky. Even though it's
still taught by too many professors. Some of the best writers
have ignored that rule for years, including you.

Jamal has it exactly right. When a rule sabotages your ability to make a point, it isn't serving you or the language. But if
breaking it—or breaking it too often—distracts readers, then
your creative license is the problem. Chances are, if you know
enough about the rules of language that you can make a case
for breaking the rule, you will have the judgment to know if
your experiment has worked.

SOME RULE BREAKERS
WHO SUCCEEDED

You don't have to butcher the language to be a rock star or poet.
Nor do you have to write about bitch's [*sic*], ho's [*sic*], or even
any body parts typically covered by bathing suits. There are
people out there writing music about original topics using correct grammar.

Consider the example of the Decemberists, a progressive
rock band that crafted an album around "The Crane Wife," a
Japanese folktale for children. From an artistic standpoint, that
idiosyncratic inspiration wallops even the most perfectly curved
backside. Then there's this lyric from their song "We Both Go
Down Together," which comes from an earlier album titled *Pica-*
resque (a distinctive term that means "relating to rogues"):

I found you, a tattooed tramp
A dirty daughter from the labor camps

I laid you down in the grass of a clearing
You wept, but your soul was willing

So, not only are they writing literate songs and performing them on an astonishing variety of instruments, they're also using "laid" correctly. They would have earned themselves a hall pass for their fine imagery even if they'd bungled this conjugation, so the care they took to get it right nearly moves us to tears, and them to the position of the official band of the Society for the Promotion of Good Grammar. (Does it hurt our argument to note that their Web site features an embroidery kit for fans? They're still rock stars, right?)

Embarrassing weeping and meaningless designations aside, there are some song lyrics, ad campaigns, and famous lines from novels and movies that are actually better for being bad.

Here's the corrected version of a passage from *Huckleberry Finn*, for example:

Pray for me. I reckoned that if she knew me, she'd take a job that was nearer to her size. But I bet she did it, just the same—she was just that kind. She would have had the grit to pray for Judas if she had thought about it. There wasn't any back-down to her, I don't think.

Here's the original:

Pray for me! I reckoned if she knowed me she'd take a job that was more nearer her size. But I bet she done it, just the same—she was just that kind. She had the grit to pray for

Judus if she took the notion—there warn't no back-down to her, I judge.

Editing for bad grammar can really suck the life out of a good bit of dialogue or narration. Bad grammar can even be necessary to great writing because it's more true to life and the human experience. Twain's idiosyncratic verb conjugations, pronouns, and modifiers certainly breathe life into his boy. Likewise, the Puss 'n' Boots character in *Shrek* is funnier because he doesn't quite conjugate his verbs correctly. (He is a Spanish kitty, after all.) "Hey!" he says. "Isn't we supposed to be having a fiesta?"

But it isn't just verisimilitude that's sometimes served with bad grammar. It can also help underscore the political point to a piece of performance art. Can you imagine if someone had edited Pink Floyd's song "The Wall"? Here's how that might look:

We don't need any thought control
Or any dark sarcasm in the classroom
Teachers, leave those kids alone.
Hey, teachers: Leave those kids alone.

The robotic feel of the edited version actually makes thought control sound appealing. Perish the thought (but not literally). By contrast, the original lyric, "We don't need no thought control," makes it sound as though the kids still have a chance of fighting oppression. To paraphrase Elvis, the bad grammar here leaves us feeling appropriately "shook up."

Perhaps the best example of "good" bad grammar comes

from an ad that wasn't even bad grammar to begin with; it was just viewed as such by people so rule-bound they couldn't perceive the deeper meaning of Apple Computer's line "Think Different."

So many purists huffed, "It should be 'Think Differently'! 'Think' is a verb, and only adverbs can modify verbs!" The ad agency that wrote this famous slogan knew that very well; the writers used it just that way in the full text of the campaign, which reads: "Here's to the crazy ones. The misfits. The rebels. The troublemakers. The round pegs in the square holes. The ones who see things *differently*. [Italics ours.] They're not fond of rules. And they have no respect for the status quo. You can praise them, disagree with them, quote them, disbelieve them, glorify or vilify them. About the only thing you can't do is ignore them. Because they change things. They invent. They imagine. They heal. They explore. They create. They inspire. They push the human race forward."

When the people at Apple urged people to "think different," they weren't saying, "Think differently than you usually do." They were saying, "Think about what it means to be different." As readers of the ad, we could infer that we should live our lives accordingly, like Einstein, Gandhi, Amelia Earhart, Jim Henson, and other geniuses celebrated in the campaign.

We can do this with language if we understand how to use it well, and if we, from time to time, "think different." More than anything else, language is a tool meant to help us change, invent, imagine, heal, explore, create, inspire, and push the human race forward. It will evolve as we do that, sometimes in annoying and surprising ways, but more often in wonderful, unpredictable fashion. As keepers of the flame, we should feel

free to honor it, play with it, and when it serves a higher purpose, shatter its rules with courage and joy.

When we do this well, the results can be thrilling. This is
something that writers and thinkers who came before knew
well. The word *grammatica* was synonymous with learning
during the Middle Ages. It was not just learning about how
language works, but also a study of mysteries contained in the
movements of the stars and the incantations of the mages. In
short, grammar was magic.

It still is. Spell well.

Bonus Material: Clip 'n' Send Letters from SPOGG

People who buy grammar books usually don't need them, except to slam down upon the heads of others (though that's not the best way to transfer knowledge inside). It's the rest of the office clowns—the ones who forward e-mail jokes and hoaxes, stand too close during conversations, and say "between you and I"—who need the refresher course on correctness.

The worst part is, the person most likely to play the role of office bungler is also the most likely to be taking home the biggest paycheck and lording his vast power over you.

To the "boss's" of the world, we address the following:

INTEROFFICE MEMORANDUM

TO: MISTER BOSS-MAN
FROM: JANE Q. SPOGG
SUBJECT: MISUNDERSTANDINGS
CC: EVERYONE IN HUMAN RESOURCES

Dear Boss,

Hey, that's a great necktie you're wearing. Diagonal stripes are slimming! But let me not waste your valuable time with petty pleasantries; if there's one thing you've taught me, it's that time is money. Come to think of it, I wish I had the time to wear fine neckties and drive a big air-conditioned sedan. That must be nice.

I am writing to let you know that I received your memo about my performance. I wanted to address some of your concerns, even offering up helpful grammatical advice I believe will save you time—and money!—in the future.

1. When forming a plural noun, there's no need for an apostrophe. When you were discussing my work "practice's," for example, you could have saved multiple milliseconds by not typing that ~~useless, stupid, and incorrect~~ punctuation mark. The same goes for your mention of my office "affair's." It's "numerous," by the way, not "numberous."

2. When you said you expected us to provide "immediate assistants" when you asked for it, I was confused.

I thought you wanted a couple of secretaries on the double, and in no way wished to cause those problems with your wife.

3. Likewise, when you said you "felt badly," I thought you were talking about some sort of hand problem. This should clear things up with Human Resources, as well as those poor assistants. I regret any dismay and/or fright I might have caused.

4. I had no idea my language offended you. When you said "fowl mouth," I thought you were talking about bird beaks. Who am I to judge one man's weird-ass phobias?

5. I brought the whiskey to the office because you said you were concerned about my "pour performance." I only meant to practice, honest.

6. When you said "wreck havoc," perhaps you meant "wreak havoc"?

7. I believe you meant to call my brain "minuscule," not "miniscule."

8. When you wrote "your fired," did you mean "you're fired"? I really hope not. I'd totally miss that necktie of yours.

Sincerely,

Jane

If it's a peer or underling with the grammar problem, then this little anonymous epistle is all you need to fix things. SPOGG offers this clip 'n' send letter, so that you can get the message across without making anyone cross—at you, anyway.

Dear _____,

Congratulations! You have been selected by the Society for the Promotion of Good Grammar to receive this note because someone cares about you and believes you will be more successful and better understood if you do the following (check any and all that apply):

[ ] Please stop using "myself" as a substitute for "me." "Myself" is a reflexive pronoun, and should only appear in sentences with "I" as the subject.

[ ] Please stop saying "between you and I." It's "between you and me," because "me" is the object of the preposition "between."

[ ] There's no need to use quotation marks for emphasis. That sign in the coffee room that says PLEASE "CLEAN UP" YOUR MUG'S should say PLEASE CLEAN UP YOUR MUGS.

[ ] Please stop saying "I just assume" when you mean "I'd just as soon."

[ ] Know the real word, not its cheap impostor. It's "supposedly," not "supposably"; "orient," not "orientate"; "converse," not "conversate"; and "agreement," not "agreeance."

[ ] Remember that "irregardless" is an irregular word, just as underwear is an irregular hat. Please use "regardless" instead (and keep your underwear under there).

Sincerely,

Your friends at SPOGG

THE OFFICIAL SPOGG PERMISSION SLIP

To whom it may concern:

(Name) _____ has permission from the Society for the Promotion of Good Grammar to (check any and all that apply):

[ ] split infinitives
[ ] end sentences with prepositions
[ ] begin sentences with conjunctions
[ ] use "like" as a conjunction
[ ] use occasional sentence fragments
[ ] say "I am good" when asked "How are you?"

None of the above will cause confusion, harm small animals, or pave the path to perdition.

Sincerely yours,

SPOGG

The Society for the Promotion
of Good Grammar

LIE AND LAY: THE PALM-SIZED CHEAT SHEET

Lie and lay often cause grammar heartburn. Relief is simple. Just put these crib notes in your wallet and whip them out the next time you're in need.

**The Society for the Promotion
of Good Grammar**

Lie: when you're talking about lying down

Present	Past	Present Participle	Past Participle
Lie	Lay	Am lying	Have lain

Lay: when there's an object being placed (such as an egg)

Present	Past	Present Participle	Past Participle
Lay	Laid	Is lying	Has laid

Acknowledgments

I can no other answer make but thanks,
And thanks. . . .

—WILLIAM SHAKESPEARE

It's a lucky thing to write a book about a subject you've adored for the better part of your life. It's an even better thing to have an enormous list of people to thank for their friendship, support, and love along the way. For someone who sits alone in an office to work, usually without benefit of a shower, I certainly have managed to collect a wonderful tribe of allies.

To those of you who have offered encouragement, insight, and spell-checking services, I thank you:

My agent, Erin Cartwright-Niumata, who persisted.

My editor, Daniela Rapp, a white-capped river of insight and humor. And my copyeditor, Adam Goldberger, who worked magic.

My students, Mae, Becky, Vidya, Maya, Zach, Paul, Stacey, Beatrice, Julia, and Jennifer, who've spent time reading, encouraging, and lifting heavy objects and medium-sized children.

My language and writing teachers, including Jon Bayley, Doug Thiel, Kathleen Mahler, C. A. Wen, David Nash, Tom

Doelger, Rob Doggett, Therese Barnette, Mike Brandon, Lindsay Heather, Judy Lightfoot, Susan Saunders, and Grey Pedersen. And to Jodi Maxmin, who lifted me up, and Harold and Barbara Levine, for keeping me there.

Professionals who reviewed chapters: plain-English expert Debra Huron, and Latin teacher Ken Van Dyke. The errors that remain are mine to rue.

My friends at Encarta: David Edwards, Jim Pollock, Bill Hollands, Jo Brown, Jeremiah Telzrow, Melissa Kruse, and others, for years of wonderful writing opportunities.

My friends who write: Nan Mooney, Kat Giantis, Emily Russin, Sumi Almquist, Elaine Porterfield, Patti Pitcher, Antonio Hopson, Jon Groebner, June Cohen, Dave McCoy, Robert Fulghum, Gerard Van der Leun, Joel Stein, Craig Conley, Sam Sutherland, James Fitch, Myriam Pollock, Bill Gruber, Jolie Stekly, Sara Easterly, Jaime Temairik, Holly Cupala, Pepper Schwartz, Barbara Card Atkinson and the Distaff group.

My friends who don't mind that I write: Kennedy and Reta, Nichole and Peter, Kat and Jim, Jenn and Kirk, Jamie and Erin, Carla and Terry, Pat and Bill, Suzy and Paul, Bill and Beverly, Elaine and Russ.

The people who help take care of my children while I write: Jennifer Durrie, Becca Hall, and everyone at Frani's, Young Child Academy, and Epiphany School. Thanks, also, to the Minnesota McClures, who took my daughters to the zoo so that I could finish the last chapter, and who also have forgiven me for many inappropriately scary bedtime stories. And thanks to the Oregon McClures, who keep me stocked in the best from Ayres Vineyard, and to Paul at Hollys', who kept me well caffeinated while I worked.

The members of the Society for the Promotion of Good Grammar, especially Barry, Jonathan, Craig, Karen, Gary, Fred, and Sue. You have been loyal, sharp-eyed, and generous with your submissions.

And finally, to my family—both the one that raised me, and the one I'm raising—I love you more than words can say, even using all available punctuation marks.

I've no doubt left people off this very long list, and for that, I apologize. You are the village, and I am the idiot—eternally grateful, despite my deficiencies.

There might be easier ways to make a living than through writing, but looking at all the people who've enriched my travels, I'm sure there is no better way to make a life.

Thank you. Thank you—and thank you!

Index